REBEL GARDENING

A BEGINNER'S HANDBOOK TO CREATING AN ORGANIC URBAN GARDEN

ALESSANDRO VITALE

WATKINS
Sharing Wisdom
Since 1893

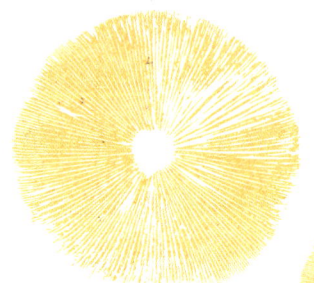

Rebel Gardening
Alessandro Vitale

First published in the UK and USA in 2023 by
Watkins, an imprint of Watkins Media Limited
Unit 11, Shepperton House, 83–93 Shepperton Road
London N1 3DF

enquiries@watkinspublishing.com

Commissioning Editor: Ella Chappell
Assistant Editor: Brittany Willis
Copyeditor: Abi Waters
Proofreader: Jan Adkins
Head of Design: Karen Smith
Design and illustrations: Alice Claire Coleman
Photography: Alessandro Vitale
Mushroom Photography: Elliot Webb
Production: Uzma Taj

Printed in Serbia

A CIP record for this book is available from the
British Library

ISBN: 978-1-78678-691-3 (Hardback)
ISBN: 978-1-78678-692-0 (eBook)

10 9 8 7 6

www.watkinspublishing.com

**For detailed videos demonstrating the techniques
I share in this book, please follow my:**

- Instagram @_spicymoustache_
- TikTok @spicymoustache
- YouTube SpicyMoustache

Publisher's note
While every care has been taken in compiling the
activities and recipes for this book, Watkins Media
Limited, or any other persons who have been
involved in working on this publication, cannot
accept responsibility for any errors or omissions,
inadvertent or not, that may be found in the text,
nor for any problems that may arise as a result
of working with the specific plants. If you are
pregnant or breastfeeding or have any special
dietary requirements or medical conditions, it is
advisable to consult a medical professional before
consuming any of the plants contained in this
book. Some activities in this book, for example
those involving different chemicals or cutting
tools, may be dangerous if instructions are not
followed precisely. Always follow manufacturer's
instructions when using tools. When growing
new plants, it is likely that you will be trying food
that you have never eaten before. Therefore,
and especially if you are prone to allergies, try
just a little first, as you would with any food. The
material contained in this book is set out in good
faith for general guidance and no liability can be
accepted for loss or expense incurred in relying
on the information given. In particular this book
is not intended to replace expert medical advice.
This book is for informational purposes only and is
for your own personal use and guidance. It is not
intended to diagnose, treat or act as a substitute
for professional medical advice. Watkins Media
Limited, or any other persons involved in working
on this publication, cannot accept responsibility
for any injury, illness or damages that result from
participating in the activities in this book.

MIX
Paper from
responsible sources
FSC® C005748

CONTENTS

INTRODUCTION

PART ONE
DEFINING YOUR SMALL SPACE

PART TWO
WHAT TO PLANT AND HOW

PART THREE
MAINTAINING YOUR GARDEN

PART FOUR
TOP PLANTS
FOR BEGINNERS

RESOURCES

INTRODUCTION

ABOUT ME AND MY GARDEN

Did you know that it's possible to grow food, no matter where you live or what space is available to you? I'm not saying this just because it's much healthier for your body and mind, but also because it will reduce your wastage and carbon footprint. In a world that is entirely detached from the origin of food and its production, I can teach you how to grow your own natural food and be in control of what you eat and how to produce it!

I'm Alessandro and I'm 30 years old. I come from northern Italy and I moved to London, UK, around seven years ago. I have loved tattoos since I was 12 years old and I work as a freelance videographer making videos on commission and also teaching people how to garden and be sustainable, reducing the amount of waste produced by your household. I personally think that if we are gardeners or in some way linked to nature, we should try to be sustainable in every aspect of our life to be true to our beliefs and preserve the environment.

My passion, though, is gardening. I've been gardening since I was a kid, and I love to see people's reaction when I tell them about my story and what I do.

"My wish is to always stay like this, living quietly in a corner of nature!"

I spent most of my life living in Italy directly in contact with a variety of fresh food. I grew up understanding not only the difference between processed food and natural food but also learning how to grow it and where it comes from.

I was inspired to start gardening thanks to my grandpa, who taught me everything he knew about our living soil and the different ways of gardening without using chemicals but instead cooperating with nature. Moving to London with my partner gave me an extra push to create an area where soil and living creatures could co-exist; a place where we could get a real sense of nature to disconnect from our daily routine.

My family is one of my main inspirations to accomplish and overcome many life challenges, thanks to my parents who offered me the chance to travel a lot during my youth and my sister who inspired me to create and preserve a better future for the younger generations. I live with my fiancée Iasmina, who is my main support and encouragement in everything I do, and I couldn't be where I am now without her and her incredible hard work.

I started growing my own food as I always felt a deep love and passion for nature, a sentiment that feels lacking in this modern society. I don't want to support the mass production of food by big companies who use chemical fertilizers and pesticides, which alter the natural biodiversity and damage the environment.

In London, I grow in a space of just 8 x 5m (26 x 16ft). However, I managed to maximize the production of food by using vertical gardening (see page 52) and any possible space available in my urban garden. This has supplied myself and my partner with enough food to avoid buying any fruit or vegetables from the stores for a whole season. I recently even turned my front yard, which was just a concrete area, into a vegetable garden. I am hoping that this book will inspire more people to have less lawn and grow more food.

I grow many types of vegetables and fruits, all in raised beds or pots. I primarily use heirloom varieties and save my own seeds. Saving seeds, or seed sovereignty (see page 75), is critical as each seed saved creates a link to the past, present and even the future.

I use many different practices to maintain a healthy soil and build a good web of microorganisms and bacteria for my plants with a regenerative approach for the land. I apply "no dig gardening" (see page 20) in order to not disturb the micro activities in my soil and follow the principles of Korean Natural Farming (see page 22), which is a cheap, organic way of farming. In addition, I also follow many permaculture principles (see page 23), which follow the belief that the ecosystems in a garden are self-sufficient and grow in a sustainable way.

The other fundamental aspect of permaculture is the notion of an optimized closed loop system. This means that everything is recycled back into the system. The design of the system ensures that waste is transformed into resources that can be reused. Processes are efficient and energy saving, requiring little maintenance.

With the principles of permaculture as a starting point, I designed my garden to waste as little as possible and try to apply

July harvest

Front yard garden

a zero-waste strategy by simply aiming to reduce, reuse and recycle wherever possible (see page 64).

I use a lot of different companion plants in my garden. Companion planting means placing different plants near one another in a garden bed for mutually beneficial reasons. This practice has many benefits and can enhance the attractiveness of your garden design by:

- adding a touch of colour
- fighting common pests
- attracting beneficial insects
- attracting pollinators
- amplifying the overall flavour of many vegetables.

Figuring out what works well together and learning about how individual plants can boost each other's growth can significantly improve productivity in your garden.

I get most of my seeds from seed swapping or online shopping with reputable companies that produce organic seeds, and every year I save most of my seeds. I particularly love chilli varieties, and I have a personal collection of roughly 600 varieties of chilli. Saving seeds is one of the most important tasks for every gardener. It allows your varieties to adapt to your own garden's specific conditions. By doing this, you have maximum control over your own food.

To save seeds is to preserve food culture. Heirloom crops wouldn't exist if it weren't for the gardeners who meticulously grew and saved seeds in the past.

"It's important to save seeds every season because a seed retains the best parts of the last year, and is a free gift for the next!"

URBAN GARDENING

Gardening in a big city like London has its ups and downs. When you live in a big city, it's often common to move from one house to another. I have had to move five times over the last seven years, which has meant planning each new garden from scratch, dismantling and rebuilding my glass greenhouse and lifting tons of soil.

In my current garden I have had a whole year without access to running water, so I had to carry two watering cans of water, holding 10 litres (2.6 gallons) each, up and down the stairs at least eight to ten times a day. I was determined to have a garden no matter what!

"There really is no planet B!"

Now that I know what can be done with many urban spaces, I'm extending my reach by creating engaging and inspirational videos about sustainability and the importance of growing your own food. I have collaborated with companies like Vans, Natwest, BBC, Unilever and many more in the hope to send a powerful message and change the way we are living.

As I always say to anyone who will listen, growing your own food is incredibly satisfying. I created a YouTube channel as my main goal is to help people create as many green spaces as possible. Soil can absorb carbon from the air, reducing carbon emissions and also reducing the amount of single-use plastic packaging you use.

Teaching people how to supply themselves with food, and sharing the importance of preserving that food to ensure that none of it is wasted, are my passions in life. Sometimes it may feel like our individual ability to create change is not possible, but it is. We can make positive changes to the environment for our future generations, even in busy towns and cities. I want to transmit my passion and enthusiasm about gardening to you, and that is why I created a book to teach you step by step how to grow a green thumb!

WHY REBEL GARDENING?

Rebel gardening shows that anyone can grow a garden of delicious organic fruit and vegetables, wildlife-friendly flowers and an abundance of herbs in absolutely any urban space with just a little bit of know-how.

It is all about not conforming and getting back to our roots. A rebel is normally someone who wants to fight against tradition but I want to embrace it and make sure our connection to nature isn't lost.

It is about looking for the opportunities to connect with nature and not the reasons why we can't. If I can do it in a rented flat in London where I didn't even have access to water in the garden, I truly believe anyone can.

We are not born knowing how to grow but we are born knowing how to naturally look after and care for things. It builds relationships and bonds and reminds me of my grandpa every time I am out in my little garden.

How funny that gardening used to be the lifeblood of our existence and now it is seen as rebellious as we are doing something so different. We're not going to the store and falling in line; we are instead experimenting and breathing life into the tiny streets of big cities.

Imagine if we all came together to do this across the world. What if we created community gardens in all of the large cities where you could simply wander around and pick produce. This is a utopian vision, but we all have to strive and believe in something. I truly believe we can, and will, change the world, and this book is helping you to take the first steps to be a rebellious gardener, too.

> "In modern society, I feel like growing your own food and trying to be self-sustaining is the ultimate act of rebellion!"

WHAT IS REBEL GARDENING?

When I started growing food in my garden, I used conventional methods, which generally involved trying to add as many beneficial things as possible to the soil and using chemicals at the first sign of pests snacking on my precious plants. I soon learned that using chemicals in the garden not only kills the whole range of insects without distinguishing between good and bad but also makes plants weaker.

A healthy, productive vegetable garden requires you to understand how to handle pests without resorting to man-made chemical pesticides, which not only keeps you from ingesting such powerful chemicals in the future but also helps you avoid pest problems in the first place.

Around 5.6 billion pounds of chemical insecticides are used worldwide each year. The majority of sprayed pesticides may be removed from the surface of fruit and veggies through washing, but some are systemic, meaning they are absorbed into your fruit and vegetables during the growing process.

SAVE THE BEES

Not only can pesticides affect bugs, but they have an impact on the entire food chain as a whole. The number of bees in the UK has significantly decreased over the past few years, along with the number of pollinators decreasing every year all over the world. All of the honey bees in the hive could be affected by pollen contamination, and it could even lead to the death of the colony. Fruit and vegetable plants cannot survive without the pollination that bees provide; therefore we appreciate them not just for their honey but also for their friendly presence in our gardens that enables everything to continue growing.

THE DANGERS OF TILLING

Tilling is when soil is turned over and broken up in order to get the ground ready for planting. Soil is tilled and chemical fertilizers are used to feed plants in industrial agriculture, which worsens the situation. Most businesses now employ chemical fertilizers to improve agricultural production since they are quick and easy to use. Because of this, soil productivity declines, streams are contaminated and air pollution is worsened, while soil hardens, organic matter is losy and pH drops.

Tilling, which is meant to prepare the soil for the next season, also damages the natural ecosystem. Tilling is a common practice for improving soil aeration, but research studies show that the risks exceed the benefits. Tilling disturbs the soil's naturally occurring bacteria and animals, which are essential to its fertility. It is these dead organisms decomposing in the soil that gives a temporary fertility. A very short-term solution!

Tilling also causes soil erosion and degeneration by releasing carbon from the soil that had been absorbed by plants. This results in the emission of carbon dioxide into the atmosphere.

Any use of chemical pesticides, herbicides or any form of tilling is strictly prohibited in my method. One way to improve the environment is to practise organic gardening. Soil regeneration and working with nature are two of my goals, which I hope will help us meet our needs for food and promote macro and microbiome diversity.

"I cultivate my organic garden in harmony with nature and strive to restore the ecosystem's balance."

Mushrooms, fruit and vegetables from the back garden

HELPING THE PLANET

Having your own growing space will not only provide you with fresh food that can improve your overall health but it will also help to reduce the negative environmental impact that our society has on the world. These are just some of the positive outcomes:

- By producing your own food, you will contribute toward a reduction in food transportation costs and air pollution, as your food doesn't need to travel far from soil to plate.
- Urban backyards and green areas also help to reduce carbon emission levels in cities, which in turn makes the air cleaner and healthier for its residents.
- Pollinators need our help. Loss of habitat is one of the main reasons why we see fewer bees, butterflies and other insects visiting our gardens. By planting a variety of native and non-native plants in your garden you help to slow and reverse the decline of insects.
- And don't forget – spending time in your own green area boosts your mental health and happiness!

"Though something like a strawberry plant may be small, growing one has the same effect as growing a tree or a forest. It can help mitigate global warming by taking in CO2, like any other plant. The difference might be small, but in a situation like ours, every little bit counts."

THE TECHNIQUES I USE

A vast microverse exists beneath our feet. It is made up of a diverse spectrum of organisms that work together with plants to help them survive and provide food. If the microverse is in equilibrium then all of the plants, animals and fungi that live in and on it are happy.

As an organic gardener, you can use a variety of strategies in the garden to work with nature and help your plants develop without upsetting the system, while also encouraging natural biodiversity of insects and microbes.

On the following pages, I will introduce you to the three main areas of gardening expertise that have together created *Rebel Gardening*. I have picked parts, techniques and philosophies from each and combined them to apply them in my garden. Together, they have allowed me to create a place where I can connect and feel at one with *Pachamama* (Mother Earth).

NO DIG GARDENING

One of my main inspirations and gardening heroes is Charles Dowding, who taught me all I know about a method called No Dig Gardening, where the principles focus on not disrupting the life within the soil.

As Charles says: "There are billions of microorganisms, known as the soil food web, down there, and they create microscopic pathways to transport water and nutrients. It's those pathways which increase soil's ability to drain excess water, while also retaining a proper moisture level." Basically, this method is all about minimizing disturbance of your garden to encourage the soil web to thrive. Any disturbance of your garden forces soil into a recovery period, which affects the natural balance in the ecosystem, and that lack of balance creates good conditions for weeds to take hold.

I have visited Charles's farm, Homeacres, in Somerset, UK, many times, and you can see the proof of this method by looking at the pathways in between his garden beds. They are weed-free and drain extremely well even after heavy rains.

Here I show how to turn any disused space into a garden ready to thrive by first establishing weed-free pathways, then raised beds where you will grow your plants.

CREATING WEED-FREE PATHWAYS

To apply this method to your growing space, if you have a lawn or weeds all over the ground, just put a layer of cardboard on top of it, making sure that the cardboard doesn't have any tape on it (if you've reused a delivery box, like me, for example!). Ink should be fine as in most cases it is vegetable ink on brown cardboard and not shiny as it often is with bits of plastic.

The cardboard acts as light exclusion for weeds on the ground, which will slowly die. The weed will decompose in a few months and the roots of the plants planted over it will just penetrate the cardboard and feed on the nutrient-rich substrate underneath. When you apply the cardboard, if you add two pieces or more, make sure to overlap them so you don't leave gaps. If you don't have any weeds and your soil is almost clean, you don't need cardboard!

Also, make sure to create an edge around your garden beds so you don't risk weeds coming back on top of the beds. You can top up this edge two to three times and you won't need to remove the cardboard as it will just decompose in about 2–3 months.

ADD A RAISED BED

You can now place a DIY raised bed on top of the layer of cardboard.

1. Begin by adding a layer of less-decomposed compost (see Note below), which is less mature and less rich in nutrients, to a raised bed. Alternatively, you could add a mix of mushroom compost, mature horse manure and/or store-bought compost.
2. Add another layer of well-matured compost, tamping it down by walking over it to make sure it's firm. While walking on it, you won't have to worry about compaction because the soil is strong enough to support the construction.
3. You could also top up with a thin layer of store-bought compost if needed.
4. Remove the raised bed sides once the compost has settled to prevent slugs from hiding in the pocket of air that is created between the compost and the sides.
5. In roughly 6–8 months, the compost level in your raised bed will fall because microorganisms eat organic waste and excrete nutrients into the soil.
6. At the beginning of each growing season, spread a thin coating of compost over the entire raised bed to provide new organic matter for the microorganisms and protect them.

The compost is organic matter that is always disintegrating, and micro- and macro-organisms are eating it and excreting more nutrients than they would otherwise if you had disturbed and disrupted these creatures' activities and the natural balance.

The soil will also increase the moisture retention capabilities so you won't have to water as much as in normal garden beds. The beauty of this method is that you can start planting your plants straight away and start growing your own food as soon as you make your garden bed.

Note:
If you don't have less decomposed compost, you can use mature compost. All you have to do is add compost to your raised beds once a year, and that's all.

JADAM NATURAL FARMING

Another extremely knowledgeable person that I have been inspired by in my gardening journey over recent years is Youngsang Cho, born in Hwaseong, Gyeonggi province of Korea. He invented a method called Jadam Organic Farming. Jadam came from a Korean phrase (*jayeon-eul dalmeun salamdeul*) that means "people who resemble nature". Its main objective is to share an ultra low-cost method of farming while also creating an environment where farmers, consumers and nature are in harmony.

The main concept of Jadam is to keep it simple and cheap. Microorganisms are everywhere. Every time you breathe in air you are breathing in microorganisms; every time you eat or drink, you are introducing them to your body; we cannot escape them unless we live in a "clean room". So when working with nature, we can naturally and easily work with these powerful organisms.

Diversity is key because the plants will call upon those microorganisms to process minerals for them. Without a large number of different microorganisms present in our growing soil, we can't be sure our plants have access to the ones they need.

Jadam does not distinguish between good and bad microorganisms, because attempting to narrow them down means a selective use of microbes, which will result in unbalanced nutrients for the plants. Instead, you should start expanding and embracing the whole biodiversity of the good and the bad microorganisms. By restoring this diversity, you'll achieve good results.

One of the most important things I learned from Jadam is to make use of what is cheap and available in my area. In particular this applies to using old plant materials to make new nutrients for my plants rather than just using them for compost. Leaf mould is one of the main things that I meticulously collect every year and transfer to my garden (see page 154).

I also learned how to make different soil and plant amendments for the garden, which I currently use to improve the soil microbiology or to get rid of pests in my garden (see page 189).

"Do not make farming an overcomplicated process but keep it simple and do as Nature does!"

—Youngsang Cho, Jadam Organic Farming

PERMACULTURE

Permaculture is the third principle behind my gardening method. Permaculture is the growth of agricultural ecosystems in a self-sufficient and sustainable way. I love this technique as it is inspired by nature – a system that works completely in synergy, based on sustainability, crop diversity, resilience and natural productivity.

The movement was founded in 1970 by Bill Mollison and David Holmgren in Australia and it really boils down to achieving our growing goals while using less energy. It uses the principles of regenerative agriculture and rewilding.

One of the main practices that helps me a lot in managing pests in my urban garden, but also helps to create symbiotic effects between the plants in my garden, is companion planting. This is when you grow specific plants close to each other with the idea that they will cooperate and thereby enhance each other's growth, improve flavour, attract beneficial insects that help to pollinate each other and prey on pests, repel nasty pests and more.

The first use of this technique is credited to the Native American Iroquois around 1600. They were planting corn using a three-sister farming method. Basically, this is when beans, corn and squash are planted together in the following way:

- Beans are planted at the base of the corn, which is used as a support for the plant to climb up.
- Beans are nitrogen fixers, which means they absorb nitrogen from the air and store it at the root level in nodules. Plants planted around beans can absorb this nitrogen whenever they need it for their vegetative growth, so while the corn helps to give the beans structure, the beans return the favour with some useful nitrogen.
- Squash are planted once the beans and corn are established, and they provide a natural mulch for the soil, which improves water retention and protects the soil microbiology.

There are many plants outside of this three-sister trio that can be planted close together to benefit each other, and I'll mention a few later in the book.

PART ONE

DEFINING YOUR SMALL SPACE

HOW TO SET UP A REBEL GARDEN

DRAW A GARDEN PLAN

The first thing you need to think about when deciding what to plant in your garden is what space you have available. A small space can be more productive per square metre than a large-scale garden, so don't let having a small space stop you from starting.

The reason a small space can work so well is that you need to be more creative and fit in as many plants as you can in order to use your growing space's full potential. It is also a great way to master how to grow certain plants from seeds to harvest and it will make it much easier one day to scale up to a bigger space.

In a space like my urban garden I wouldn't plant anything that grows too tall or that takes up too much space. I grow varieties that are relatively small so I can fit as many different varieties as possible in a small area.

If you are lucky enough to own a drone, you could fly above your growing space to get an idea of what you have available and also its exact shape. Failing that, you can go on google maps and look at a satellite image of your garden. Knowing its shape (which is likely to be irregular) and taking measurements on the ground means you can draw it out and plan things like raised beds.

Take your time to do this properly as it will really pay off in the long run. I know it can feel hard at the start, when you are full of excitement, to not just run out there and start planting, but you won't be making the most of your garden and it will lead to you being frustrated later.

WHERE IS THE SUN?

The sun is key to growing and you need to know where it is in terms of your garden space. Keep an eye on the sun rotation over your garden for a day or two to get an idea of the areas that are more, or less, exposed to sunlight. Ideally, do it for a bit longer if you can contain your excitement, so you really get to understand your garden. Make sure you consider some margin of error because the more that we get into spring and summer the coverage of the sunlight changes slightly.

Colour code your plan to make it easy to see the best planting areas. Grey out where the shade is on the plan of your garden and use yellow or orange to show where there is direct sunlight. This way you can choose the plants that will thrive best in these conditions or put things in place to help – basil can be protected from the direct sunlight by planting taller tomato plants next to it to act as a shade and stop it getting sunburned, for example.

Front yard in July

GROWING FOOD IN THE SHADE

A great advantage to growing in small spaces is that you can use the shade to your advantage to benefit plants that grow well in shade. If you grow cucumbers vertically in a trellis like I have done, you could potentially grow lettuce in pots and move them around in the summer following the shade created by your trellis. This is a bit like people sitting around the pool on holiday, chasing the sun or the shade as the sun moves.

This is also a great way to grow lettuce, as most gardeners struggle in the middle of summer when it sits in direct sunlight causing it to bolt and go into flower. Thanks to your small space you can grow things that people with larger spaces will struggle to grow. You just have to be mindful of how the sun moves.

You can grow many other things in a shady area, such as parsley, mint or oregano. I also plant radishes all around the base of my cucumbers so that they are shaded by the huge leaves and the tall trellis.

There is so much different information online telling you what you can grow and where in your garden. I get people asking me all the time what they can grow in the shade, particularly in urban areas as they are likely to be more shady.

There is so much opportunity, even if the harvest won't be as high in yield, you can still produce tasty food. So don't be scared about experimenting and trying to plant things that are not supposed to be grown in shade. You might actually be surprised at what can be harvested in a shady area.

I keep going back to this, but planning really is key to getting the most out of your small space.

BEST VEG TO GROW IN A SHADY SPOT

The most common vegetables that can be grown in full or partial shade are leafy brassicas, which can include kale or pak choi (bok choy). Plan ahead and plant them in any shady areas of your garden.

Kale

CREATE A PLANTING SPREADSHEET

Once you have a plan on paper it is time to decide where and what to plant in your garden. This is the fun bit! You could create a spreadsheet from scratch or you could go online and look for a template. While the dates for sowing your seeds might change every single year, having a basic plan gives you a reference point to start from.

Your spreadsheet should be an easy way to show and understand the basics:

- what to plant
- when to plant it
- where to plant it

Don't forget to mark in your seed growing time if you are starting from seed versus plugs.

I usually start seeds indoors four to six weeks before the last wave of frost. Seed starting times are calculated by taking the date of the last frost and subtracting the number of days until the transplant. However, the seed packets will normally tell you how many weeks, so check the information on the packet.

Be careful not to get too excited and start seeds indoors too early. You will become overwhelmed by plants in need of transplant without having enough space or time. If this does happen, reach out to people locally and see if anyone wants to swap and give you some plants later in the season. The community element of gardening really is inspiring and exciting and something I believe we all could do with embracing.

CHOOSING WHAT TO PLANT

The first thing to try and ascertain is how much of the vegetables and fruits you intend to plant you and your family will eat throughout the year. There is no point planting lots of spinach in your garden and growing a high yield if the only person who likes it is your Auntie Maura who lives 200 miles away. You could of course swap produce with neighbours or other local growers, but there is nothing like the satisfying feeling of wandering into your garden, basket in hand, and choosing ingredients you love to make a delicious dinner.

A few things to keep in mind:

- Remember that plants like tomatoes, squash, pepper and aubergines (eggplant) keep producing throughout the season, which saves a lot of time and garden space.
- Try to avoid growing something just because it looks cool in the picture on the seed packet. It is fun to experiment, but be realistic in what you choose. Maybe you want to grow some electric daisies to give your sorbet a kick. They are something you can't normally buy in shops or are expensive to buy but are really fun and inexpensive to grow. They create a fizzy sensation on your tongue when you eat them – some

people say it is like licking a battery – but not everyone likes them.

- If you are growing because you want to eat more organic food, but also realize that you don't have much time to spend in the garden, try to grow things that are low maintenance and almost pest-free, such as garlic, onions or herbs.
- It is important to be mindful of the time you have to harvest. There is no point planting redcurrant bushes if you are not going to have time to manually pick them all and also preserve the high-yielding crop. They will end up being food for the birds. Unless of course you want to feed and attract lots of birds to your garden so you can sit and watch them with a mug of coffee.

You may be growing to save money so I would recommend that you go to the supermarket and check to see what is the most expensive vegetable that you could grow based on your climate and consider growing those. Remember to be mindful about what your local climate will allow. There is no point identifying avocado as your biggest spend and trying to grow them in central London. As much as you want to, it isn't going to happen.

If your main aim is to save money and feed your family, plant produce that is highly productive like courgettes (zucchini), tomatoes, aubergines or peppers. In any case make sure to check what grows best in your area but also do a few experiments.

Accepting that fruits and vegetables have a season makes you much more open to not eating the same food all year round. Changing your thinking from "I want to create this recipe therefore I need this produce" to "what do I have available to create a recipe for dinner?" is a definite shift in behaviour and it won't happen overnight. If you are able to embrace the change, you will find a new excitement in the changing seasons and what food will soon be available.

See later chapters (pages 212–67) for more information on specific fruits and vegetables to get more ideas for your small garden.

BE A NOSY NEIGHBOUR

I like to go and see what neighbours are growing in their gardens and what is working well for them. You could knock on their doors and chat to them, or if you are in the UK you could make use of National Association of Gardening days, when people open their gardens to the general public. These are great community events as people really love to talk about what they have done and show their gardens off. You may also have a community garden near you. There are hundreds dotted around the UK and they are an absolute treasure trove of local information.

Courgette, annual plant

Rhubarb, perennial plant

ANNUALS VS PERENNIALS

An annual plant means it will only flower and grow once and then die. Though you can of course collect and save the seeds to grow next season.

A perennial will grow back each season as long as it doesn't get killed off in the frost or you have someone who is over zealous in their weeding and clears them up when they are in their dormant stage.

You also get biennials, which are plants that flower every two years.

You will need to work out which of the plants on your garden plan are annual plants, and which are perennial.

In an ideal world it is a good idea to have a mix of both in your garden. The perennials cut down on the amount you need to grow from seed and plant each year. However they normally have a shorter growing season, versus the annuals that flower for longer.

Perennials also like to be planted in spring and fall, so if you miss that window of opportunity you need to wait to get the best crop versus an annual that you can sometimes even plant in the height of summer depending on the variety.

It is important to show some patience with perennials. You can think you have failed the first year as you don't get that hit of dopamine from their bumper crop but as the years go on their yield can increase and you will be glad you had the patience to wait.

Annuals also give you a chance to mix up what you plant in your garden. Some things won't work as well as you thought or you may find you want the opportunity to grow a new and exciting crop.

The most important thing is to have fun and mix it up. This is your space and you can do what you like!

PROTECT YOUR GROWING SPACE

Now you have done most of the planning for your garden, you need to think about how you will protect the plants you have chosen. This will make sure they have the best chance of survival. Remember, not everything you plant will grow, even if you do everything within your power to make it happen. We can't control every seed and that is part of the joy of nature.

You will need to protect your plants from the elements, which include frost, rain as well as too much sun. Also knowing your soil chemistry will really help. You will learn more as you go along but here are some tips and tricks to get you started.

FRUIT CAGES

If you are growing dwarf trees or fruits (see page 115), you may want to protect your fruit with fruit cages so the birds don't come and steal your wonderful bounty. There is nothing worse than thinking I will harvest that tomorrow and wandering outside to see it has been decimated.

The cons to cages are firstly, aesthetics, how it looks. Unless you like the industrial prison look, they can be quite ugly. Also they can be difficult to reach inside and get to the produce.

Another option is to attach bright ribbons and bells to your trees to scare the birds away and protect your crop. This isn't always foolproof but you can experiment with what works for you.

NETTING

You can use different types of netting to protect your veg and fruit from birds and natural garden pests, such as foxes or aphids. You can also use beneficial insects and crop plants to do this (see pages 173–94). You don't have to spend lots on netting either. While there are lots of pre-made options available on the market, you could make your own from recycled materials and things your neighbours or friends don't want anymore.

CLOCHES

Cloches aren't just used to keep food hot; they are also used to protect and help cuttings and seeds to grow. Cloches retain heat from the ground as well as create a microclimate, which is perfect for seedlings as they germinate, also protecting them from the birds. They are great if you have a small space like a balcony or a garden that doesn't have room for a greenhouse.

They are also a much cheaper way to get started. They used to be made from glass but now they are made from a rigid transparent plastic, not the most sustainable thing but it could last for many years. You can pick them up quite cheaply from garden centres or even secondhand. You could also make your own DIY cloches using recycled materials, such as cut down plastic bottles placed over the top of plants, which has the benefit of being completely free and better for the environment.

GREENHOUSES

If you have the space, a greenhouse is a great way to protect your plants and help them grow when germinating seedlings. It protects plants from all the elements, from frost to wind, and gives them a safe haven to thrive in before you take them outside. It also makes the most of the natural light and traps the heat inside.

Some plants that need a different climate to grow should be kept in a greenhouse at all times. You just need to make sure you water them as they don't get the added benefit of rain. Don't let not having space or the money for a greenhouse stop you from starting to grow though.

POLYTUNNELS

Like greenhouses, polytunnels create spaces with higher temperatures and humidity, allowing you to grow all year round. The definition of a polytunnel is a polythene covered frame. Similar to a cloche they offer really good protection and are pretty quick and cheap to put up depending on the size you want. You can make them yourself too, which really does keep costs down.

COLD FRAMES AND MINI GREENHOUSES

A cold frame is a box that lies flat on the ground with a glazed sloping lid. Mini greenhouses are glazed boxes that stand vertically with openings on one side.

It is harder to control the temperature in them as they are such a small space but they are an excellent space-saving alternative to harden off your cuttings in the spring. They can also be a great home for crops such as aubergines and tomatoes in the summer to encourage growth, increase yield and provide a bumper crop.

You can also use them to overwinter veg ready for next year. You are likely to want to add some extra warmth – bubble wrap can be great for this. Again, ask friends if they have had a delivery and have some spare bubble wrap that would otherwise end up in the bin. This should prevent winter frosts from killing overwintering crops.

STRATEGIC PLANTING

You can plant produce together that works in harmony as nature intended. Some plants will attract insects like lacewings or hoverflies and act as pest control (see page 189).

SCARECROWS

These can sometimes work but often you see birds sitting on them as they become used to them in the garden. So if you do set up a scarecrow it is important you move it around your garden and don't leave it in the same place. You also want to add clothes to it that will blow in the wind. You could create your very own DIY arty scarecrow.

You will need to protect your
plants from the elements,
which include frost, rain
as well as too much sun.

Tomatoes and melons under cover

GROWING SPACES

HOW TO OPTIMIZE SPACE

When you start growing it can feel overwhelming knowing where to start and what to do. Planning can really help with this. We have talked about mapping out and planning your garden, working out where the shade and sunlight is and how to maximize the crops you grow in these areas (see pages 27–30).

It is not about packing as much into your garden as possible with no thought though. Growing vertically in your garden is key to making the most of the space you have available in small urban gardens (see page 52). Always look up, and see what space you can use. Equally, succession planting can be important in small spaces (see page 122). Firstly, I want to talk about the often overlooked front garden, as this is key to making sure you maximize your food production.

Growing food on different levels

MAKING THE MOST OF YOUR FRONT GARDEN

I noticed lots of front yards are not being used, or worse still are being used, not as growing spaces, but to store old junk. I want to inspire you to create your own space in your front garden. You could even do this if you live in a shared block of flats with little space or you could create this on a balcony.

I set up and created a community garden near my home in London using my front yard, where people could come and help themselves to veg and herbs at no cost to them. It felt great to do something for my community but I had to limit the amount of people accessing the garden as some plants have been completely ripped out of the ground, damaging the other plants. You could even put a sign up and tell people to help themselves as they're passing. Start with just a few plants, and then plant more each season so it feels manageable rather than overwhelming.

First of all, go and look at items that people don't want that you could use as containers; these could be old tyres, plastic containers, anything that is deemed as trash to someone else but could be useful to you. Ask your friends and neighbours or knock on someone's door if you see something outside discarded in their front yard. The local tip is also another good source of materials. You might be surprised by the amount of materials you could find by simply walking down your road.

You will need a few materials to hand that will really help you to maximize the space:

- plastic sheet or cardboard
- trowel
- staple gun with staples
- scissors
- stanley knife
- secateurs
- leaves and green materials (lawn mower clippings, pruned twigs and small branches – that kind of thing. You can always ask around your neighbourhood if you don't have any).

Your upcycled containers will probably need to be lined with plastic if they are going to hold compost and plants. Alternatively, use cardboard if you have bare ground available (see pages 20–1). I recommend you cut a bigger proportion of plastic than the surface you need to cover. You could use a plastic sheet or some old tarp, whatever works for your container.

Using Tyres

There is no need to staple the plastic inside because once you fill the tyre with soil, the weight will do the job for you, but make sure to line it with plastic or materials to avoid chemical leakage in your soil.

Using Wood

If you are making wooden containers, like one made from old pallets or crates, you could fill it up with soil and organic matter without any liner inside. However, you can also line it with plastic to retain moisture. If so, follow these instructions:

1. Start by stapling the sides and then proceed to the corners around the upper border.
2. Once you have stapled the corners, just fold the plastic inward and staple it.
3. Cut the excess plastic away with a stanley knife or with a pair of scissors.
4. Use the stanley knife to cut some holes at the bottom of your planter as you don't want any stagnant water.
5. Fill up the bottom of your container with green material; you could also use kitchen scraps or coffee grounds (ask your local coffee shop) to give a boost of nitrogen to the plants. I use a peat-free compost and put this on top. I also add some organic nutrients like insect frass or mykorizae to enrich and promote the life of my soil.

"Paint and design your DIY balcony or front garden space to make it look cool and very much your own."

RAISED BED GARDENING

There is nothing better than wandering out into your urban space, however big or small, and picking your fruit and veg, creating a spontaneous dinner just for yourself or for friends and family. And I promise you that you don't need to spend a fortune in order to do this. There are many different cost-effective ways to do it so that gardening can be a fun and life-changing activity with minimum expense.

People are always asking me how much it costs to make my urban garden. There is often an expectation that the cost of materials such as timber and good-quality compost make it prohibitively expensive. Luckily for you I have some great ways to save money and one of these are through raised beds.

Raised beds are central to my garden because there are so many benefits to them. They allow me to grow in areas that would otherwise be impossible, they have great drainage, are easy to irrigate, while reducing the amount of watering needed.

Some gardens may be too marshy and wet, have the wrong or contaminated soil, or even, like mine, be covered in concrete. Raised beds are an affordable and relatively easy fix for these issues. When growing in a raised bed you can add your own choice of compost and soil, which means you can control any potential contaminants as well as the soil's nutritional content and pH levels.

Raised beds trap in heat so they can offer longer growing seasons, which means you can plant some of your veg earlier than if you planted it in the ground.

While the beds won't fend off any unwanted insects and pests, they will slow them down.

As they need to climb that extra distance, you have time to stop them in their tracks or add in the great aphid eater – the ladybird.

As well as reducing strain on your back while you plant, weed and maintain them, raised beds will make your veg more accessible, especially to those with disabilities, eliminating any restriction as to who can enjoy your garden. It is great to see more councils making public allotments accessible to all through their raised beds.

Not only are they practical, but they look great, too! They can make your garden look much neater and tidier. They keep your veg confined to one space and you will be able to control exactly how and where things will grow, something that can be quite difficult when growing them from ground level.

However, a wooden raised bed could be the perfect hiding spot for slugs and snails in the pockets of air forming between the soil and the sides of your raised bed, but with a bit of prevention and control you can avoid too much damage.

WHAT MATERIAL SHOULD I USE?

Building a tall raised bed can be expensive depending on the materials used, but it doesn't have to be! I have built some of my raised beds from scraps I've found lying around, but doing this could take a bit of extra time, particularly if you are not really into DIY. So I have some quick, cost-effective solutions for you depending on the material you want to choose and the amount of work you want to put in.

Different materials can help control the temperature, have different durability, make building them easier or more of a challenge and of course change how your garden looks.

Metal

While they can look quite unappealing, unless you like an industrial look in your garden (although nothing a lick of paint won't fix!), metal raised beds are becoming more and more popular due to their high durability, affordability and low maintenance, as they don't rot, swell or shrink with moisture (unlike wooden beds). You can purchase a ready-made one or make your own using corrugated metal sheets and a metal or wood frame. Regardless of your decision, make sure the metal is galvanized – this will ensure that it doesn't rust.

Wood

Traditionally, wood is the go-to raised bed material and it is viewed as the best option and the one I always choose. While it's often cheap, the lower value options won't always last as long. They are often susceptible to rotting and general wear and tear. If you do opt for wood, then cedar is a very solid choice as it is resistant to rot and moisture. If you decide to seal the wood (which isn't necessary with the likes of cedar), then make sure to pick a non-toxic sealer!

That said, a great, cheap way to build a wooden raised bed would be to go to your local DIY store and ask them for a palette collar – most of the time they will give them to you for free or for a very cheap price. If you can't find any, have a look online and you can often pick them up cheap or people give them away for free if you are able to collect them.

Palette collars are stackable and you can build your raised beds to different sizes depending on your needs. I would start with just two to have an ideal raised bed. They are also foldable so are easy to store at home until you are ready to start. I also use an old lumberjack technique like my friend Jack suggested, which is burning the surface of the wood so it lasts longer.

Bricks/Rocks

If you're up for a challenge then making raised beds out of bricks is a great option. More preparation is needed in terms of the ground being level and evenly measured out as you need to take into account the extra length mortar will add to your sides. Depending on your choice of materials, bricks can be very costly, but their long life does make up for this. Be wary of what you use, as soil will absorb anything it can.

HOW BIG SHOULD THEY BE?

This all depends on you: what you're growing and might want to grow. If space isn't an issue, then you can always build more when needed, but if it is then you want to get this right the first time.

Take into consideration what you will grow in each bed and how much room each plant will need to grow healthily. My rule of thumb is a minimum size of 39cm (15in). You want to be able to easily reach the middle point with ease. If they're too wide, you will struggle to give sufficient care to all of the plants and you'll make things harder for yourself.

WHAT CAN I GROW IN THEM?

Some veg will need to be in a raised bed to ensure that it has good drainage, which is good if what you want to grow doesn't require much water or if your land is waterlogged. Here are a few ideas to get started with: courgette (zucchini), kale, cucumbers, lettuce, radishes, spinach, tomatoes, peas, onions, peppers and herbs.

WHERE TO PUT THEM

Sunlight is key when choosing where to build raised beds as you won't have the choice later on to move them. Not easily anyway! Monitor when the sun hits your garden, where and for how long. Do this for a few weeks. It can feel frustrating waiting when you just want to get started but it will make a difference in the long run. Some veg need more sunlight than others to grow so take this into consideration, too.

One last thing to think about is what might grow there. If there are parts of your garden that are prone to being infested with weeds, either make sure they're permanently dealt with or place a layer of cardboard on the ground before building your raised bed, which should kill and slow the weed by light obstruction (see page 20).

CONSTRUCTING YOUR RAISED BED

First off, clear the area where you are going to be building your bed(s). Make sure all grass, stones, weeds and other debris are cleared. Once this is done, cover with cardboard to prevent any weeds from poking through later.

For wooden raised beds, measure out where they will go and mark them out by putting a wooden post on each corner: one between each corner for the short sides and two between each corner for the long sides. These are what you will screw the sides to unless you are using the palette method. You can watch my video on YouTube to bring the palette method to life.

For stone or brick beds, create a level foundation and ideally have a layer of bricks below ground surface to provide a suitable foundation for you to build upon. Use mortar to join the bricks together.

Once you have the structure of your raised bed done you can start covering the insides with a protective sheet.

I used plastic sheets that a friend gave me for free but you could also check building sites close to where you live. They often just throw them out so it can be a great free resource. I know plastic is not the most sustainable choice but it will last for a really long time and if you can get it for free it's just a win-win. If you have soil under your raised bed you could just leave it, too.

If you are using a plastic sheet, staple it all in and then make some holes at the bottom so you have drainage.

WHAT IS THE CHEAPEST WAY TO FILL A RAISED BED?

Before you go out and spend a load of money, check the quality of the soil on your land; you may find you can use that to add to your beds.

There's a few things to look out for, which will indicate whether your soil is already suitable for growing in. The main thing to look out for is whether the soil is well draining (meaning water runs through it). So it shouldn't be too heavy or clay-like and equally it shouldn't be sandy either.

After you have established that the soil's characteristics are suitable, check for any leftover rubbish in the ground and if you find any, I'd make sure to sift the soil with a sifter and remove it all. You could also test the pH of your soil. It is claimed that vegetables grow best with a pH of 5.8 to 6.5. You can buy test strips for as little as a few pounds or invest in a pH pen.

I don't have any soil in my garden, except for a small section that is about 2m (6½ft) wide, so I use a few different

techniques to fill my raised beds including the Hugelkultur method, which is a great and affordable way to fill raised beds especially in cold temperatures.

Hugelkultur is a German word that means mound culture or hill culture. Don't worry if you pronounce it wrong. I am Italian with an English accent – I have spent a lot of time researching it and learning to pronounce it right, and I am still not convinced that I do!

Hugelkultur is very simple. It involves burying lots of rotting debris beneath the soil, such as sticks and logs. Ideally, apple branches are great for this technique. The larger the pieces you use, the longer they'll last. Add grass cuttings, leaves and whatever else you can find that will decompose into the gaps between the logs, then add the soil on top of it. What you are doing is mimicking the process that happens in a forest every year.

Normally, in a raised bed, the roots will grow into 40–50 per cent of the depth, which means 50–60 per cent of your raised bed isn't being used. This is where Hugelkultur comes into play and you can save a lot of money. It is nothing more than filling up the bottom layer of your raised beds with rotting food and wood.

This is great for your raised beds as it creates a lot of nutrients, organic materials and air pockets beneficial for the roots of the plants you are going to plant in there. There are so many other benefits too that happen throughout the year – the bottom layer becomes rich and full of soil life, as the food shrinks its air pockets.

During the first few years the decomposing food will warm up your soil and extend the growing season. When you dig a hole and bury some food, it holds nutrients, especially carbon, which is available for the plants you plant over it. It acts like a carbon sink and is called carbon sequestration.

Also, because Hugelkultur holds so much water, it can be a great way to grow in dry areas like a desert without applying any sort of irrigation. Just make sure you aren't using cedar wood as it is full of lots of natural pesticides and fungicides. The same goes for black locust and black walnut, as they contain natural organic compounds that can resist rot for a hundred years or more, so keep them for your fences as they could be really toxic for most plants.

I use local branches from my local woods, trying to mix sizes to fill up the bottom parts of my raised beds, but you could also use grass clippings, unfinished compost or old plant material.

Once I have placed all the wood materials at the bottom of my raised bed, I fill all the holes with spoiled hail (treated straw). You could also use unfinished compost to fill up the holes. One of the benefits of compost is that it retains water, but once the wooden pieces have decomposed they turn into huge sponges and are going to retain a lot more water than compost. This in turn means that you will need to water your raised beds less, which is always a winner!

You can then walk over your raised beds in order to compact them down. Or if you have kids, why not get them involved, encouraging them to run over the bed. It will really make them feel part of it! Make sure there are no holes left and it is packed down.

Start adding the well-rotted, nutrient-rich compost on top and finish with good-quality soil. You can choose something cheap or create your own mix. If you use a cheap mix from your local garden centre mix 2.5cm (1in) of perlite with every layer of soil to add better drainage; just make sure it is organic and peat free. Leave a couple of inches at the top so that you can mulch the top layer once all the plants are planted.

Remember during the first year of your raised bed, the level of your soil will decrease due to the wood at the bottom decomposing – like a forest floor would. Microorganisms will feed on the organic matter, transforming it into nutrients. So you just need to top it up twice a year with compost and mulch and slowly you will build the perfect soil structure for your plants. Making your own compost recycles old plant material and creates free food for your future plants.

Compost is always a good option although not the fastest one. If you have long-term plans to make raised beds,

then get a compost heap going right away (see page 126). If not, it's always worth having one to top up your beds with and of course it's entirely free and great for the environment.

As with pretty much everything, soil is much cheaper in bulk. If you have a lot of beds to fill and want to save some time, then buy enough soil in bulk to fill them all. Or why not join up with some friends to do it en masse.

Deconstructed Hugelkultur concept

YEARLY MAINTENANCE

Weeds are always going to be an issue, even in raised beds. Even if you start with none, seeds will eventually end up in there as birds visit your garden. So make sure to keep on top of them. The earlier you get to them, the easier it'll be to get rid of them – or eat them if they are tasty weeds, such as dandelions or nettles.

With wooden raised beds you want to keep an eye out for weathering and general wear and tear. Look out for any rot. If you happen to find some defective wood, it's possible to replace it without too much trouble, although this probably won't happen.

Brick beds can get damaged in the winter due to temperatures dropping and rising above freezing constantly, so as temperatures start to rise each year, check over the beds to ensure there are no cracks or other damage that needs fixing.

DIY BED COVERS

Covering raised beds isn't 100 per cent necessary, but it can be a good idea. It makes sense as you spend the whole year ensuring the beds are kept in good condition, so letting winter have its way with them when they could simply be covered, doesn't seem like the best option.

It is also a great way to provide extra food for the winter months as having a covered bed extends the growing season. You don't need extra skills and you don't need any DIY experience to make a raised bed cover. It really is very simple.

There are lots of vegetables you can plant at the end of summer and the beginning of autumn depending on your climate; from carrots to winter spinach to leeks. The key to a successful winter harvest is knowing what vegetables to grow and pairing them with the right season extenders. This means growing cold-tolerant crops in structures like cold frames, polytunnels or greenhouses (see page 35). You could buy a pre-made tunnel or make one like I have from scratch trying to use recycled materials as much as possible.

It's important to understand that the growth of most vegetables slows down as the daylight hours shrink to less than 10 hours a day. This happens for me in London around November time. So I need to make sure that most vegetables reach a good size before this happens. At this point, my cold-tolerant vegetables stay tucked in, inside my season extenders, waiting for me to harvest them and eat them.

You don't need anything fancy, just something sufficient to protect the soil from the harsh winter winds. This will allow the microbes to continue working throughout the cold months, ready for spring. Also, soil doesn't need to rest. It is a living thing and could constantly have plants growing in it. A good idea would be to never leave bare soil exposed but always cover it with high-density plants like mustard or other leafy greens. This will help to carry on the carbon sequestration effect, adding organic matter to the ground for the microorganisms to eat and expel as more nutrients, and also improve the soil structure.

PREPARING BEDS TO BE COVERED

Before you start covering anything, there's a bit of prep you'll have to do in your raised beds to reduce your wastage and promote optimal growing conditions for your plants.

Firstly, cut all the plants left over from the previous season at the base. The reason you don't want to take the roots out of the raised beds is because they will slowly decompose and turn into nutrients for the microorganisms in your soil. They will also feed the plants that follow.

There is a micro universe underneath your soil and every time you dig you will disturb the micro- and macro-organisms. Plants interact with mycelium (a fungal network), creating symbiotic relationships (see page 92). This creates a healthy ecosystem in your soil, which helps your plants to thrive. Every time you dig, you disturb them and potentially damage them. It is amazing what goes on and in our soil – nature is rather marvellous.

Make sure you don't throw away your leftover plant material. You can use it for many things – you can add it to your compost to turn it into new nutrients for your plants or you can add it to your worm bin to feed your worms (see page 135). Or you could even create new fertilizer by adding the plant material to a bucket and collecting some leaf mould from an area with high vegetation and adding rainwater or unchlorinated water (see page 154).

The only other thing I do before planting my cold-tolerant crops is add around 3–5cm (1¼–2in) of homemade or store-bought compost to the raised beds before planting. This will be an ideal new home for the plants rich in nutrients and microorganisms. Think of it as a house-warming present!

HOW TO MAKE YOUR RAISED BED COVER

Now you need to protect your raised beds, and the cheapest and easiest method I have found to cover my raised beds is with my own homemade PVC tunnels. For the below materials, you can ask your neighbours or friends if they are throwing anything away or look to see what building waste you can see in your area. It's worth looking at your local tip. One person's trash is another person's treasure.

You will need:

- 1.5cm (½in) thick PVC pipes, as they are really flexible and ideal to bend and create a frame
- Long bits of timber to use at the top to join all your arches together and create a solid structure
- Some metal saddle pipe clips to secure the PVC pipes to the sides of your raised beds (make sure they are water resistant)
- Transparent plastic sheet to cover the raised beds – it is really important to make sure it is transparent as you will need light in there to grow your vegetables!
- Cable ties or metal wire to secure the plastic sheet to the frame
- Tape measure
- Marker pen
- A staple gun with staples would be helpful

DIY raised bed cover

DEFINING YOUR SMALL SPACE

1. Firstly, you need to decide on what kind of plants you will be planting in your raised bed, because you need to make it tall enough to fit your plants. It would be very annoying if the plants didn't fit due to poor planning!

2. Measure the length of the raised bed and mark with a marker wherever you want to put the arches. I would suggest you put one at either end of your bed, no matter the size. I used four arches when I made mine, so I marked four different spots where I was going to put the arches to support the structure of my cover.

3. Repeat the process on the other side of the raised bed, making sure they are matching. I used a tape measure to make sure it was exact.

4. Drill in your metal saddle pipe clips on each mark you have made on your raised bed, making sure not to drill all the way through as you will need some space to fit your tubes. I used the inner side of my raised bed because it is really close to the fence, but you could also of course do it on the outer side. It is all about maximizing the space you have.

5. Cut the PVC tube into sections, making sure they are all the same length. Fit one end of your PVC tube into your pipe clip and secure it in place by drilling all the way through the clips. Repeat this process until complete.

6. Place two timbers vertically, one at each end of the raised bed, so it becomes a much sturdier structure for the plastic sheet that will be placed over it. Attach them to the raised bed by screwing them in at the bottom.

7. Place a piece of timber horizontally between the two vertical timbers and attach it to the PVC arches with cable ties or metal wire.

8. Add the plastic sheet – this is a really easy process. The only thing to remember is that the sheet needs securing in place. You can either do this by stapling the sides in place or adding some bricks to hold it down. Just make sure one of the sides is left open or you won't be able to access what is inside – you will need access to be able to tend to your plants, water and harvest them.

If it helps to watch it visually as well you can watch my video on my YouTube channel about how to do this and of course ask me any questions there. I am always happy to help.

VERTICAL GARDENING

When it comes to gardening, it's not the size but how you use it that counts.

You don't need a big space to grow food; it's all about utilizing the space that you have available. Trying to grow lots of different varieties in a restricted space risks a small harvest. You are not allowing the roots to develop to their full potential due to the competition with all the other plants, restricting their growth.

Most people starting a garden tend to grow plants horizontally using rows, raised beds and pots. Doing this ignores the fact that walls, fences or even stairs around your garden could be used to maximize harvest in a small space. Also it is a great way to add beauty, character and charm to your growing space. However, if you don't like the idea of drilling your walls or fences there are still many other ways to build a vertical growing space by using super affordable materials in a few easy steps.

There are many reasons why growing vertically is a great idea. Not only will vertical gardening help you to maximize your growing space and therefore your yield, it's great for the environment, better for your back and it looks so cool. Also, as your plants are off the ground with better air circulation, they are less susceptible to disease, rot and fungi. Better air circulation also means that more air is being purified by the plants, so that is great for your lungs, especially in an urban environment. It is also possible to save water, as you can simply water the top layer and let it trickle down so none is wasted.

Peas and mange tout

CREATING A VERTICAL GARDEN

Once you discover the hacks and tricks to vertically gardening it will open a whole new way of growing in your garden and utilizing your space. It's not difficult to picture. Adding a few plants will transform the area into a place that attracts pollinators, and you'll be able to provide your neighbours and friends with fresh fruits and vegetables.

Although it's possible to attach pots directly to walls and fences, it is advisable to use a structure like a trellis or a frame to hang them from and also support your plants so you have two functions in one. It is very easy to build your own and it's a great way to recycle and repurpose old materials.

I love DIY, so I made my own 120 x 100cm (47 x 39in) trellis in my raised bed to support my plants. When I got started, I mapped out my project on paper so I could visualize it and understand what materials I would need to make the trellis. I then sourced all the materials from the DIY store, but you could find them secondhand or sometimes for free, although if you want a vertical garden that will last over the years, I do recommend you invest in good materials.

The size of your raised bed may be different but the technique is the same. So you need to adapt this to the sizes you are working with! The frame I built was 180 x 86cm (70 x 34in) and I used timber I bought, which was 2cm (¾in) thick, 3.8cm (1½in) wide and 180cm (70in) long.

1. Begin by building a frame, starting from the two sides that are 100cm (39in). To get started, put your timber on a flat surface. Measure 86cm (34in) between them and cut them to the right size, arranging them into a square frame. I used a hand saw to do this, but you could use power tools if you have them.
2. Put some wood under each corner so it makes it easier to drill the holes. Drill a pilot hole to prevent the wood from splitting. I use screws that are 3.5mm (⅛in) thick and 6cm (2¼in) long.
3. Once the wood is joined, add one bridge to every corner to make sure that the structure is sturdy. This is your first side completed.
4. Repeat this step to create another side.

5. Bang in small nails to the whole perimeter of the wooden frame at 12cm (5in) intervals. Don't bang the nails all the way in as you will use these nails as anchors for threading and weaving a cotton thread (I used nails with a slightly bigger head to make this easier).

6. Next, weave the trellises with thread, first vertically, then horizontally. You should end up with a square shaped pattern. Avoid using thread containing polyester or plastic; instead opt for 100 per cent cotton thread, as it is biodegradable and better for the planet. Copper wire is an alternative, but I find the plants tend to get tangled in it, and cotton can just be snipped away and composted at the end of the season.

7. Once all the sides are done, use an electric drill to attach the base to the raised beds. I made two trellises, so I attached one to each side, but you can put them wherever you have space. You could of course hammer the trellis straight into the soil, but I find this technique works really well as it offers much more resistance and support.

8. For even more support, I measured the distance between the two sides and attached two wooden pieces at each end. You can now run thread on top to create an extra frame or you can just leave it and use the two sides to grow your plants.

9. Plant climbers at the base of the threads and intertwine them as they grow. There will be plenty of space for them to grow and for you to harvest the crop.

For the base of my raised bed I used fallen branches I collected from the local woods. If you see any sign or rotting or fungal activity on them it's still good as that means the decomposing process has already started and you will be collecting some indigenous microbes and transporting them to your garden (see page 85).

WORK SMARTER IN THE OPEN AIR

Tasks performed under the calming influence of nature are performed much better, with a greater accuracy, a higher yield and a higher quality result.

BALCONY GARDENING

Even if you live in a high-rise flat it doesn't mean you can't grow anything meaningful. Even the smallest of balconies can be used to grow a variety of organic vegetables. Your neighbours will be astounded at what you can produce in your small space and you might even inspire them to try their hand at a bit of growing, too.

SUNLIGHT

There are some things to consider when planning your balcony garden. Firstly, which way is it facing? If it faces north (in the northern hemisphere), then it will be in shade all day. On the other hand, if it faces south, it will get a full day of sunshine. If it's east or west, you will get sun for some of the day, and you may want to think about being able to move your plants.

The amount of sunlight you get is important when thinking about what things you can grow. Also, it is worth remembering that if you are high up it may be a little colder and windier than at ground level. This shouldn't be too much of a problem, but it might slightly shorten your growing season, and if it's particularly windy you might want to choose more low-growing veg, like carrots rather than tomatoes.

POLLINATORS

Another thing to consider are pollinators. If you live on the tenth floor, it would be hard for bees and other beneficial pollinators to reach your balcony garden and pollinate plants, so it's always good to check and manually pollinate your plants if needed. To do this you just need to use a brush and move pollen from one flower to the other, making sure you don't do it using different varieties of plants or you might end up with cross pollination.

SPACE

The next thing to think about is your available space. Remember that you might need to get out onto the balcony to maintain, water and harvest your crops, so you will need room to move around. And don't forget that you are not limited to the flat surface – the walls and balustrade will make great growing areas (see page 52). You can also make the most of hanging baskets or make your own using the DIY hanging containers (see page 64). They can be expensive at garden centres but you can pick up damaged ones for a few pounds that often have the plastic lining missing or a broken hanger. You can fix them for next to nothing using plastic bags and twine to hang them with. They are a great way to get the most of your small space and repurpose old materials.

Even if your balcony is south facing, with plenty of sunlight, it is worth planting your balcony garden in containers. Not only can you move them about depending on where the sun hits, but they are more manageable and you can bring them inside in winter. You can also use window boxes as well as trellises and even a small teepee. You should position your pots so that the smallest and lowest are closest to the front, so they don't block the sun from those behind.

CONTAINER SIZE

Do remember that when plants are fully grown and bursting with produce, they will be quite heavy. Try to use lighter materials when choosing your containers such as recycled or donated plastic, and avoid heavy terracotta pots if you can.

WHAT TO GROW

When choosing what to grow on your balcony, don't just think about what you want to eat, but also consider what is likely to thrive in the space you have. Vines such as tomatoes, peas and green beans are great for vertical spaces like the balustrades and trellises. Larger pots are great for bushy vegetables like chillies and peppers, or small fruit trees, like gooseberry or redcurrant.

Strawberries, raspberries and other similar plants love growing in hanging baskets and window boxes, as do many herbs and leafy greens like lettuce or spinach. Other vegetables like Swiss chard, carrots and even potatoes can be grown in containers or even compost bags and can do well on a balcony. Ask any neighbours what they have had success with and don't be afraid to experiment.

One last thing to remember is to plant companion flowers as well as fruit and veg (see page 12). It's not likely that the bees and butterflies got the message that you have started growing high up so you may need to advertise. Also, flowers like nasturtiums and marigolds not only look great, but will also attract and trap any pests so they won't eat your lovely veg. You can create a real showstopper of a planting space that you are proud of and want to venture out to see every single morning. Be a "rebel" and reclaim your outside space.

Plants growing on a balcony

When choosing what to grow on your balcony, don't just think about what you want to eat, but also consider what is likely to thrive in the space you have.

ROOFTOP GARDENING

If you have access to a flat roof that is being underused, it could make a great sun-trap of a garden, where you could potentially grow just about everything. While it is possible to completely cover a roof with soil and turn it into a "green roof", this could be expensive and takes a lot of planning.

A few important things to consider

- Is the structure strong enough to take all that extra weight?
- Do you have permission from your landlord?
- How are you going to get all that soil up there in the first place?

Luckily, you can still have a beautiful rooftop garden without doing anything too drastic, which will produce a huge variety of food, relatively inexpensively. Ultimately, a rooftop garden is very similar to a balcony, but you are likely to have a little more space and sunlight. It is well worth spending time observing your rooftop for sunny and shady spots and planning what you want to grow and where. If there is no shade, you might want to put up some sort of shelter.

SPACE

Things you will need to think about are your access to the space; if you have to climb out of a window to get there it might be difficult to bring large, heavy plant pots with you. Can you get a hose to it or will you have to carry watering can after watering can through your home? It might be worth installing a water butt and thinking about minimizing the watering you need to do.

VISIBILITY

Your rooftop might be visible from other buildings nearby. If this is a problem, you might want to think about some sort of screening, perhaps a fence or some potted trees. This could be done with a trellis with vines growing over it.

STORAGE

Storage on a rooftop might also be a problem. It is likely to be difficult to build a tool shed on top of your house. A fence panel with an array of hooks and a set of bookshelves could be a solution, perhaps with a tarp covering to give it some protection from the elements. You may also want to store things like seeds, compost or fertilizer. An old school locker or a filing cabinet could work well and you might be able to pick one up cheaply online. Also, bench storage is a great idea for doubling usage of available space.

RAISED BEDS

Raised beds are a possibility on a rooftop, as well as any of the vertical gardening techniques discussed previously (see page 52). When planning a rooftop garden, like any garden, think not only about the growing you are planning to do, but how else you might want to use the space. Would it make a cool, unique spot to have a barbecue or drink cocktails with your friends? Could it be a quiet, tranquil place you can relax in, listen to music or catch up with some work? This is not only going to influence the layout of the garden, but its aesthetics, too. It's a place you will spend a lot of time in, so make it your own.

LOOK AROUND

If you live in a city it is worth going to visit some rooftop gardens locally to see what they grow and to get inspiration when designing your space. The possibilities are limitless and you can create something so special. Alternatively, there are a lot of great pages online of people using their rooftop in the most creative ways.

Plant only what you eat!

WINDOWSILL GARDENING

Believe it or not but you can grow a whole host of things on your windowsill, and not just in your kitchen, but all over your flat or house. You may have no garden – or you may have a huge garden, but still want to grow even more. There really is nothing that can get in the way of getting started. Imagine yourself plucking fresh lettuce from your windowsill in the depths of winter. It will also reduce your plastic usage, your reliance on shopping at the grocery store and will save you money.

From microgreens to herbs to beautiful edible flowers, there is so much goodness that you can grow inside all year round. It is really easy to do, it looks great, and having green plants in your home will also clean the air. So what is stopping you getting started?

There are a few things to consider before you get started!

LIGHT

A southwest-facing windowsill will get the most light but even a west-facing windowsill will give you plenty. Even if you live with another wall blocking your light, you still have options.

You can also show your plants a little love by buying an LED or COB light to help them grow and switching it on for extra daylight hours in the depths of winter to encourage them along.

HEAT

If you have double-glazed windows your plants will be nice and toasty all year round, but if you have old windows make sure you plug any gaps or holes so they don't get chilly. You just need something long and thin like an old cotton t-shirt that you can cut into strips and stuff in the gaps.

If you want to create a little humidity for your plants you can add a tray of pebbles to the windowsill and add some water to them. This also makes a good secure spot for your containers to sit in.

CONTAINERS

Long and thin containers are ideal for filling windowsill spaces, or jars and secondhand plastic pots, even plastic bottles cut in half. You could even make yourself a DIY self-watering pot (see page 166). Make sure your container doesn't overhang the windowsill though as it will become unbalanced and you could end up with soil in your breakfast.

Just as with growing outside, you need to make sure your containers have good drainage, so make sure any pots you use have drainage holes in the base to avoid them becoming waterlogged inside. You will also want to put a tray underneath to catch the water that runs off.

ADDING NUTRIENTS

One thing that indoor plants won't get naturally like they do outside is nutrients from the soil. So you will need to make sure you add some organic fertilizer and homemade or peat-free compost.

My ideal mix is:

- 40 per cent organic compost
- 40 per cent peat-free soil
- 10 per cent perlite or vermiculite
- 10 per cent worm casting.

I also like to nourish them with organic plant food once the substrate nutrients are exhausted.

Viola plants growing in a repurposed water bottle

CHOOSING WHAT TO PLANT

Now you can start to think about what to grow! You need to consider if the plants you have chosen are self-pollinating, as you are unlikely to get any visiting bees in your house and the wind won't be inside to aid pollen movement. You can help them along by using a toothbrush, or even a small paintbrush or cotton bud, to scrape off the pollen from inside a flower and transfer it to another flower.

There are so many options! Don't try to do them all at once. Gradually add to your windowsills all over your house and experiment and have fun with it!

Culinary herbs
Rosemary, oregano and thyme work really well and they definitely make dinner or a cocktail more interesting.

Kale and other veg
Dwarf varieties, such as Dwarf Blue, work well. It is really worth exploring what dwarf varieties of vegetables are out there. It is a whole new world of food that you won't find at the grocery store. Spinach is another great green to grow and have to hand, and once again you won't be buying those plastic bags of it. There is something really special about being more self-sufficient.

Edible flowers
A double bonus as they will add beauty to your indoor space and you can also eat them. There are so many to choose from; it is surprising how many flowers are edible. Did you know geraniums are? And that different varieties have different flavours? Just double check they are edible before you grow them and pop them in your mouth.

Lettuce
Grocery stores sell grow-at-home lettuce plants that stay fresh for longer but what about one that you cut back and it grows back, meaning you don't have to buy it ever again from the store? You can spend what you save on new plants, as once you start you will be hooked. More and more plants seem to be entering my living space. It definitely makes me happy.

Tomatoes
Will grow indoors all year round. Yes, you read that right, you can have a constant supply. You can grow them in little pots, although it can be hard for them to make it into the salad or your dinner as they are just so delicious. They always taste more flavourful and delicious when you grow them yourself. Micro cherry tomatoes are a great one to grow, but do think about your lighting. They are likely to need a little extra help especially in the winter months.

Chillies

One of my personal favourites, so I am going to advocate growing these in your home. They look great, too, as they add a splash of colour to your home and heat to your dinner. I would definitely recommend starting with something easy like jalapeño, sugar rush peach or, if you are a fan of deep, dark-coloured plants and peppers, you can't go wrong with black goat weed. If you are planting them in the winter when the light is low, again, make sure to add some lighting or they won't develop any fruit.

Spring onions (Scallions)

You can simply place them in water and just snip off what you need as and when you need it. Again, another great saving as you won't need to buy them and they keep coming back.

Carrots

Did you know you can even grow carrots on your windowsill? Again you want to go for a smaller variety. The benefit to this is you can even eat the lovely fresh green tops, which are often chopped off when you buy them. Whizz them up with some nuts, lemon juice, olive oil and vegan cheese and, hey presto: a vegan pesto.

Ginger

One thing that is hard to grow outside in the UK is ginger, but it can actually thrive on your windowsill, especially if you have put stones down to create some humidity. Imagine growing your own ginger; it could be a perfect combination with your chillies.

Peas

You could train them up your window and let them really take over and frame the space; like having a fancy living vegetable wall in your home. You can snap off some peas and pop them straight in your mouth.

This isn't an extensive list but I wanted to get you excited about exploring the possibilities of what you grow at home! I would love to see what you do in your windowsill spaces. So follow me on Instagram and Tiktok and make a video to show me what you have done in your growing space. You will inspire others to follow suit as they see what can be achieved on your windowsill. Just be careful if you have cats as they have been known to knock over a pot or two in my house!

UPCYCLING CONTAINER IDEAS

Here are a few ideas for creating containers or pots for your small garden.

 ## DIY HANGING POTS

Recycling materials to use in my garden has been one of the main goals to create a sustainable space in the middle of the city, ever since I started growing food in an urban space. However, not everyone has a garden and this is why this DIY hanging pot is a great way to grow food on a balcony or terrace, by simply recycling plastic bottles of any size.

You will need :

- 2 x plastic bottles (I used 5 litre/1.3 gallon bottles)
- Pyrography pen (for poking holes in the plastic. If you don't have a pyrography pen, you could instead hold a nail with some pliers, heat it on fire and then use it to poke the holes)
- Compost mix
- Natural twine
- Seeds or plants

1. Cut off the top part of the bottles, around the shoulder. Remove the cap and make holes for draining half way down the top part of the bottle.
2. Make four holes around the top part of the body of the bottle opposite each other.
3. Make two holes at the bottom for drainage (keep a 3–4cm/1–2in gap from the bottom)
4. Put the neck of the bottle upside down inside the body of the bottle and push it to the bottom.
5. Fill up with compost and plant your chosen seed or plant.
6. Cut two natural twine pieces of the same length. Run one piece through two holes of the same bottle and two holes of another bottle and repeat on the other side.

TIP: If using clear containers, paint over the bottom to protect the delicate roots from sunlight. However, if you live somewhere where it is super hot, it could be an idea to put white cloth around them to help reflect heat and stop the roots heating up in the midday sun.

DIY VERTICAL GARDEN

This is a cheap way to make a vertical, indoor or outdoor, garden using transparent plastic bottles.If you don't drink soda or buy bottled water, ask your friends and family to save theirs for you, or put something in your local social media group. It is surprising how helpful people can be. They also get to feel good about reducing their waste. You may even inspire others to do it, too.

It is a great way to save on water as well, as the water is recycled for every layer. You just water the first layer and it flows down to the one below with no waste.

The perfect time to do this is when spring is just around the corner. It is a great time to start planning and organizing your garden, balcony or whatever space you have.

You will need:

- A 25mm (1in) flat wood drill bit
- 10 x 2-litre (½-gallon) plastic bottles with lids
- Hammer and nail
- Cutter or stanley knife
- Clay pebbles, rocks or stones
- Acrylic paint of any colour
- Tape measure
- Drill
- Staple gun
- Staples
- Marker pen

DIY hanging pots

REBEL GARDENING

1. Use the drill bit to drill a hole at the bottom of 5 plastic bottles. Use the centre of the flat part at the base of the bottle as your guide. Please be careful! Use your fingers to pull out any rogue plastic and make it smooth.

2. Place the bottleneck of one, undrilled bottle through the drilled hole of another bottle, slotting them together so you have 5 double bottles to make sure they fit. Make sure you keep the plastic caps as you will need them later.

3. Use the hammer and nail to poke holes in the plastic caps – this will become the drainage for your vertical garden. Use something like a vice to keep the plastic caps in place – don't use your hands as you could make a mess or injure yourself. Make many small holes for the drainage.

4. Grab a marker pen and draw a square on the front, bottom half of each of the plastic bottles.

5. Use a cutter or stanley knife to simply follow the lines you have drawn and cut out the squares of plastic.

6. Screw on the plastic caps to the bottle tops inside. This will keep the bottles in place and act as drainage.

7. Staple the bottles to a fence or a trellis, or whatever surface you have available. I like to use a tape measure to mark out the right placement for each pair of bottles so it is even and visually appealing. I like to alternate between one pair of bottles being slightly lower than the adjacent one, going up and down like this to give it a more appealing look.

8. When you are happy with your markings, you are ready to start fixing the bottles in pairs. Put them on so the bottles are upside down, with the flat base at the top and the neck of the bottle at the bottom. Make sure the side with the cut-out square hole is facing you on all of them as you need access to this to grow your plants.

9. Put some clay pebbles or rocks/stones at the bottom of each bottle so you have better drainage. Add soil – you don't need to add too much because once you transplant you are going to top it up.

10. Paint the bottom of the bottles to protect the roots from sunlight. I recommend two coats of white acrylic paint, which works pretty well on plastic.

SIZE UP

I build this same system with 5-litre (1.3-gallon) bottles and it works just as well as the smaller ones, if not better. All you need to do is to replace the flat wood drill bit with a bigger one of 32mm (1¼in) and follow the process as explained above.

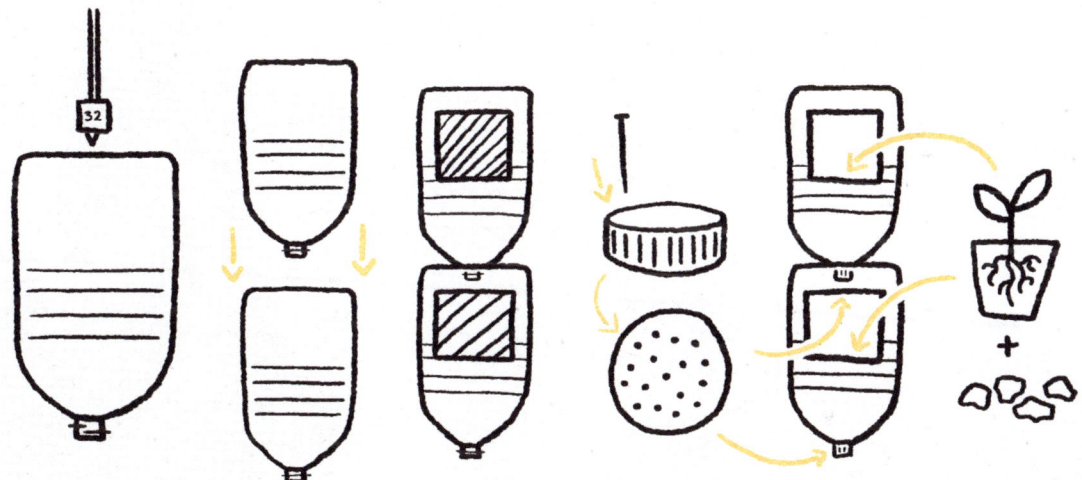

What plants should I use?

You can use cloned plants (for example, strawberry runners), seeds or transplant small plants bought from a nursery. These can be anything from herbs to fruit or flowers; just make sure they aren't too heavy for the bottles.

With any plant you should make a bit of space in the soil in the middle of your bottle and pop them in. Make sure your plant is facing outward otherwise it will just grow upward to meet the sun and you may not get as good a yield as it is putting its energy in the wrong place. Put some soil over it and I also recommend adding mulch to retain water, but it is of course an optional extra.

Water just the top layers and the water should drip down. If it doesn't you can just adjust your drainage cap by opening it or closing it a bit more.

This is a great way to maximize space and increase the harvest in your small space. There are lots of other ways out there to do something like this, but the most important part for me is to recycle. If we all do tiny bits it can lead to big change.

PART TWO

WHAT TO PLANT AND HOW

GROWING FROM SEED AND TRANSPLANTING

DIFFERENT TYPES OF SEEDS

Whether we use them to grow cereals, herbs, fruits or vegetables, seeds are an important part of our lives. However, because of the many names and abbreviations used to categorize each different variety, there is a lot of confusion about the different types of seeds that you can find in stores nowadays.

The classification of various types of seeds can be based on the shape of the seeds, their use or the plant that will grow from the seed.

Seeds are necessary for plant growth because they allow plants to reproduce. Some plants, however, produce spores rather than seeds, which are used to propagate the species.

Because there are over a million varieties of seeds, it is difficult to isolate a specific type of seed.

When looking through a vegetable seed catalogue, pay close attention to the specific needs of each plant and whether or not you have the proper growing conditions. Also consider the length of the harvest; it is critical to time your harvest to coincide with ideal growing conditions, otherwise your vegetables may perish before you can harvest them.

A small tip for obtaining seeds is to exchange them online or through social media. Many social media platforms, offer a variety of groups in almost every country where seed collectors can chat and swap rare varieties.

It doesn't matter what kind of seed you're looking for, the most important thing is to choose healthy seeds. GMO seeds, hybrid seeds, organic seeds and heirloom seeds are the four main categories of seeds.

GMO SEEDS

Genetically modified organisms (GMOs) are species whose genes have been manipulated by humans. Nothing could be more certain than the short-term benefits of GMO seeds for the food supply. But the long-term ramifications of such a practice are still up in the air, according to several experts.

For those considering purchasing GMO seeds for their gardens, the answer is that it's not possible. GMO seeds are not available for purchase by home gardeners. Even if you really want some, you won't be able to get any. GMO seeds are only sold to farmers after they have signed a contract outlining the conditions under which they may use the seed. Such an agreement between seed firms and homeowners will not be signed.

Several elements of GMO seeds remain a mystery, including the danger that GMO crops could contaminate non-GMO crops. Wind, insects, evading cultivating plants and improper handling of non-GMO crops all have the potential to infect non-GMO crops.

The genetic makeup of GMO seeds has been altered as a result of human intervention. A plant is injected with genes from a different species with the expectation that the advantageous gene would be passed down to the plant's progeny. The practice of altering plants in this manner creates ethical considerations. Be careful not to confuse genetically modified hybrids with genetically altered seeds.

HYBRID SEEDS

These are when one plant variety is crossed with another in order to produce a new hybrid. In cross-pollination, pollen from one plant's male flowers is used to fertilize the female flowers of another. After pollination, the female flower's ovary begins to grow and develops into a fruit. When those fruits ripen, the seeds they contain will be hybrid seeds. A hybrid seed is an attempt to combine the best characteristics of both parents' genes.

I experimented with this process with chillies by hand-pollinating with a brush and gently brushing the inside of one flower onto another flower of a different plant. One of the things that you'll notice is the SHU changes (Scoville Heat Unit, a scale to determine how spicy a chilli is) due to the combination of two different varieties of chillies. However, It takes many generations to have a stable hybrid and not every chilli could be hybridized with a random variety. For a hybrid to be stable, a plant will have to produce the same fruit over years without changing shape, flavour or any typical characteristic after the pollination. I have managed to collect over 500 different varieties of open pollinated chilli plants by exchanging and buying seeds online.

When it comes to hybrid seeds, they are referred to as F1 varieties (Filial 1 – literally "first children" or first generation). Farmers tend to not save these varieties of seeds as they won't breed true. This means that the seed will likely not produce plants that are true to their type.

Plant breeders make a lot of crosses and keep meticulous records of the outcomes until they find a combination that consistently yields superior results, are more resistant to pests or presents a few improvements compared to the previous generations. This procedure might take a long time to complete. However, by sourcing F1 varieties, you will rely entirely on a seed company as you won't be able to save the seeds. This takes away part of your autonomy and has more control over seed sovereignty.

ORGANIC SEEDS

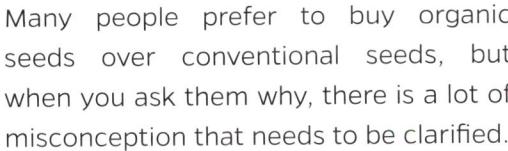

Many people prefer to buy organic seeds over conventional seeds, but when you ask them why, there is a lot of misconception that needs to be clarified.

From a scientific perspective, the phrase "organic" refers to material that was once alive, as the term "organic matter" itself states, but from the perspective of certification, there is a lengthy list of specific standards. They all follow the same rules when it comes to organic food production, and organic companies are obliged to conform.

Some people believe that organic seeds are those that have not been subjected to any chemicals during the growing process. This is not totally accurate, as they may be exposed to harmful organic compounds. They can be employed at higher quantities than synthetic chemicals because of their poorer efficacy. This isn't to imply that organic seeds are bad, as they are actually one of my favourites, but we need to dispel this common misconception.

HEIRLOOM SEEDS

An heirloom is generally considered something worth passing down. As a result, an heirloom seed is one that has been carefully produced and saved over the course of many generations because it is considered particularly valuable.

The flavour, productivity, hardiness or adaptability could all be reasons for its worth. There are several family heirlooms that have been passed down for over a century. Some of them have a history that goes back as far as 300 years. These seed varieties have proven their worth to many people and families for a long time by being stored and saved for so long.

Heirloom seeds are one of my favourite choices for my own garden. For years, I've been on the hunt for new types to add to my ever-expanding collection. Heirloom seeds are kept in numerous seed banks across the world. Genetic diversity is safeguarded in a seed bank by storing seeds for the future. Seed vaults are usually flood-, bomb- and radiation-proof, and contain jars of seeds from various plant species. For the most part, seeds are stored in cold, low-humidity environments. As a result, they are better preserved and will continue to grow in the future.

Across the globe, there are more than 1,000 seed banks, each with a unique mission and scope. Around 40 per cent of the world's plant species are at risk of extinction, according to estimates. A seed bank serves as a type of insurance, allowing us to save as many species as possible from extinction. I had the opportunity to visit a seed bank in Coventry called Garden Organic (www. gardenorganic.org.uk) to learn how important seeds are for the future of humanity. I highly recommend visiting them if you are in the area.

Storing seeds organized by names

Seeds from Urban Farmer

SEED SOVEREIGNTY

Saving seeds is one of the most important tasks for every gardener. Gardeners are able to take back control of their own food supply in this way. It is important to save your own seeds each year so that your variety can adjust to your environment.

To maintain food traditions, it is important to store seeds. Without the gardeners who diligently nurtured and conserved seeds, heirloom crops would not exist.

Saving seeds is also essential to preserve food sovereignty. To put it another way, seed sovereignty is the right of farmers, gardeners and other food producers to keep and use, breed, exchange and sell open-source seeds. Genetically engineered, patented or seeds controlled by a company are not considered to be "open source".

The present worldwide problems of COVID-19 and climate change have increased the importance of food sovereignty as a means of empowering communities toward self-determination and sustainability.

The worldwide COVID-19 pandemic has disrupted supply lines and made many of us realize how reliant we are on distant systems that are beyond our control. For a more sustainable future, it makes sense to save seeds and produce your own food. Using, storing and passing on seeds is a good way to ensure their long-term viability and your own independence.

HOW TO SOW SEEDS

When you first start talking about gardening, you will hear the term sowing or seed sowing many times. Sowing is simply the process of placing the seed in soil to germinate (sprouting from the ground) and grow into a plant. This is where everything begins. I have many people asking me for tips on sowing seeds, so here are my essential tips.

HOW TO PREPARE A SOIL MIX

When planting or transplanting a plant, the first thing you need to do is prepare a proper soil mix. To guarantee that you are providing the plant with all the nutrients it needs, as well as proper drainage and aeration, you need to use a rich soil mix that includes compost (see pages 125–38).

A typical soil mix for conventional gardening would include 50 per cent potting soil, 40 per cent compost, 10 per cent worm castings and a few handfuls of vermiculite or perlite. Mycorrhizae should also be included in the mix if available (see page 92). Fungi and plants establish symbiotic interactions called mycorrhizae. Increased water and nutrient absorption is provided by the fungi's colonization of the host plant's root system. Fungi get carbohydrates from photosynthesis in return for their services.

But don't worry if it all seems a little complex and overwhelming to you at this point in time. Instead of using seeds the usual way, I encourage you to switch to one that is more in tune with nature by combining the no dig strategy (see page 20) with the simple act of growing your plants in compost.

Most of the plants in my garden grow and produce a lot without the addition of additional nutrients from the compost I use. Not digging and not tilling will leave soil undisturbed, so the mycelium will have an opportunity to grow and expand beneath the surface, forming the crucial symbiotic relationship that aids in decomposition of organic matter and the delivery of basic nutrients to your plants. Microorganisms handle the rest of the work by devouring old roots and organic matter and developing new nutrients in my raised beds once a year, which is all I need to do.

Leaf mould for a soil mix

SEED STARTING

Starting seeds inside is an excellent way to get a jump on the gardening season. It's not difficult to cultivate plants from seed to harvest, provided you have the necessary lighting and equipment. Keep things simple and don't make gardening an overly complicated activity. When people ask me for advice, this is usually the first thing I say.

Starting with just a few types is recommended because each plant has a unique set of seed-starting requirements. In terms of ease of germinating seeds, marigolds, tomatoes and beans top the list. Some other great choices for beginners are herbs like basil, broad beans (fava beans), calendula, nasturtiums and leafy lettuce. Before handling the more difficult seeds, such as carrots and aubergines (eggplant), start with the less fussy ones, such as tomatoes.

You should use an excellent seed compost or an all-purpose potting soil while you're planting seeds. I would always favour using my own organic compost. However, if you can't have your own ready on time or you are not sure about the quality, there are some great options to purchase, such as Morland Gold.

The best soil

It is best to use a finely textured soil when planting seeds. To encourage your seedling to emerge into the light and begin producing its own food, a fine and uniform consistency is required. Although the seed has only a tiny quantity of nourishment to aid in its rise to the surface where it can receive light, if your soil is too hard, it will build barriers that force the seed to grow around and finally die before it can emerge from beneath your garden soil. This is why I recommend soaking your seeds in FPJ (fermented plant juice) for a few minutes to provide all the minerals and nutrients as soon as the plant breaks the seed husk (see page 150).

Screening or filtering:

My local garden centre had a sifter for sale for a few pounds. Or, with a few pieces of wood and a stapler, you can make a square frame and attach some metal mesh to it. You should fill trays to the brim, pressing the soil down into the plugs with your fingers to ensure that they are solid before adding a new layer of soil. Plants like a well-drained, firm soil for their roots to flourish in.

REBEL GARDENING

Planting the seeds:

Using your fingertips, you can now make small holes on the surface and put your seed and/or seeds into them. Make certain the holes point in the appropriate direction but don't be too fussy about it. Almost every seed has a pointed end and a more rounded end, which you may have never noticed or known about before, but you will from now on! Because the seed's rounded end is its "top", the pointed end should always be placed downward. Remember that beans and a few other seeds have their pointy end on one side, so make sure you plant them so that the roots may grow down. However, if you've already planted your seeds and haven't followed these instructions, you shouldn't be too concerned. Roots will find their way down and the plant will emerge from the ground in one way or another.

Protect your seeds:

Cover the seeds with a thin layer of the same substrate that you used in your trays, pots or ground to protect them and create ideal conditions for germinations to happen. Using your hands, gently sweep the tray's surface to ensure that all the seeds have been buried. As an alternative method, you may simply spread another layer of soil over the top using a strainer to ensure that it is equally dispersed, which is great for encouraging seed germination and removing the big pieces of soil that could obstruct plants emerging from the ground.

Labelling:

Label your trays or pots with the name of the plant and the date you sowed it.

Watering:

Watering the trays with a watering can or hose pipe fitted with a fine rose is the best approach to avoid disturbing the seeds too much. To ensure that the potting mix is evenly saturated, repeat this step several times until the tray or ground is completely saturated. Keep an eye out for water damage in trays and pots on a regular basis. Lifting them up will reveal how much moisture is present in the potting mix. If the plant feels light in weight, it means that it will require water. You may also use a reservoir to water the plants thoroughly by placing the trays in the reservoir and waiting for the drainage holes on the bottom of each tray to soak up the water. Remove them as soon as you notice that the surface has become moist. As an alternative, tiny plants can be watered from the bottom to avoid stressing them too much.

SOWING SEEDS UNDERCOVER

With a greenhouse, cold frame or polytunnel, you will be able to get a head start on the growing season. When the weather is still bad outside, you can protect your seedlings from cold winds and pests by sowing them in a greenhouse. As a result of its ability to store solar energy and release it in the form of heat on sunny days, greenhouses and other similar structures have the potential to advance the start of the growing season by as much as a month or more.

Buying a greenhouse could be expensive, but there are ways around it. I bought mine secondhand; by adding up the cost of renting a van, driving there and collecting it, I spent just a few hundred pounds for something worth in the range of thousands. If you're a very keen gardener like me, I highly recommend monitoring secondhand platforms, as you can find really good deals. Alternatively, you could easily build your own without any specific DIY skills.

Another easy and cheap way to sow undercover outdoors would be to cover a pot with a small sheet of plastic and secure it around the pot by using an elastic band. This will help to maintain ideal moisture and temperature. You could also cut a plastic bottle in half and poke a few holes for the air. Use it to cover your plants in the ground and protect them from cold, wind and rain.

SOWING SEEDS DIRECTLY

Direct sowing is one of the easiest ways to start seeds in your garden. It just means that you are sowing seeds directly in the area where you want your plant to be, rather than starting them indoors and moving them out, or starting them in trays and transplanting.

However, this technique will only be successful if the weather and sowing time are taken into consideration.

You will need to get the timing right to sow at the right time, which should be when the last wave of frost is long gone and the soil temperature is good enough to welcome new seeds. As a rule of thumb, you can start sowing a few hardy varieties outdoors like beetroots (beets), turnip, radish, a few varieties of leafy lettuce, parsnip and broccoli at least three to four weeks after the last wave of frost. You can easily find out the last wave of frost by visiting your local nursery and asking people working there or check online. However, be aware that these are only rough references, which won't take into consideration any microclimate or variations due to climate changes.

The type of seed you are sowing will have a significant impact on the spacing you use when direct seeding. Overcrowding your seeds will cause them to compete for light and nutrients, so leave at least 1cm (½in) between each one as a safety precaution. In the event of overcrowding, plants develop only one or two flowers and immediately begin the process of seed production. This is not the case if you are using a technique called multi-sowing (see below). If you are sowing really small seeds like carrot seeds, just grab one pinch of around 30 seeds (no need to be too precise) and quickly distribute them in one rapid sweep. This is much more effective than planting each seed individually and wasting hours to try and sow them properly.

Once they begin to grow and reach 2.5cm (1in) in height, you will need to apply a technique called thinning. This means you will have to remove each tiny plant germinated every 10cm (4in), leaving the strongest looking. Once removed, discard them by adding them to your compost pile or worm farm. This will stop them from competing and stealing food from each other.

SOWING SEEDS IN MODULAR TRAYS

If you are sowing vegetables and flowers in big quantities and you want to give them a head start either indoors or undercover, sowing in modular trays could be the best choice for your needs. Modular trays are seed trays divided into rows of individual cells, so that each seed has its own little space to grow.

Modular trays are the perfect way to start seeds while there's something else growing in the ground and do something called succession planting. This means that there's no waiting time between one crop and another and you continuously harvest and plant new things throughout the season. Soil, contrary to common opinion, never needs to rest and it's good to keep it planted out throughout the whole year, even if it's just a cover crop with the sole purpose of accumulating carbon into the ground. To succeed in succession planting you need to be careful with your dates and timings. Buying a sowing calendar helps me every year and I highly recommend purchasing either the Maria Thun Biodynamic Calendar or Charles Dowding Vegetable Garden Calendar.

Another pro of using modular trays is the protection that they offer from slugs and snails by raising the seeds from the floor. Most modular trays also include domes (plastic or other kind of covers), which help to maintain humidity and temperature, creating ideal conditions for the germination. My favourite seed trays are designed and sold by Charles Dowding. They are more pricey than a normal seed tray but they will last a lifetime as they are solid plastic, durable (you can actually put your weight over them and they will hold it just fine) and with bigger holes at the bottom, which helps to easily pop out a plant when it's time to transplant it.

You could also use something called multi-sowing when you are using modular trays. I learned this technique from Charles Dowding and it works for many different varieties of seeds like basil, beetroot, chard, chervil, coriander (cilantro), dill, parsley, fennel, kale, leek, onion, peas, radish, rocket, spinach and turnip. This technique comes with a variety of benefits and I use it every year to sow many of my seeds.

- It helps you to save time in sowing as you don't have to separate seed by seed.
- It saves compost as you will use less to propagate the same number of plants.
- It saves space as you can grow more plants in a small area.
- You will also have some sort of companion planting effect, as Charles, over his 40-plus years of organic gardening, noticed how plants like to grow with their "friends" in clumps.

You plant three to eight seeds (depending on the variety) in a single cell and transplant them out when ready. Plant them outside at the recommended spacing for one plant, and they will grow in clumps. Make sure you don't sow too many root vegetables in the same cell or you will have more leaves compared to roots.

Trinity dwarf french beans

Modular seed trays designed by Charles Dowding

SAVING SEEDS

Saving and storing your own seeds is one of the most satisfying and empowering tasks in gardening. It gives you the satisfying feeling of a closed loop when you manage to grow a plant, harvest the fruit, compost the greens and save the seeds.

When you decide you want to save the seeds of a specific plant, you can either leave a few of its fruits, vegetables or flowers to over-ripen (past the mature picking time) on the plant and remove the rest, so the plant can preserve energy to continue to grow, or you can just leave them all on the plant and check them regularly until they are ready to be picked and used for seeds.

The most common and easiest seeds to save are flower seeds. Marigolds are a good example – don't pick the flowers when they finish producing; leave them on the plant to dry. Once fully dry, you can harvest the flower head by removing the outer petals, and the seeds within can be used in your garden next year.

The easiest seeds that I'd personally recommend saving as a beginner gardener would be tomatoes, peppers, beans and peas. This is because self-pollinating blooms and easy-to-store seeds are the common features of these plants.

Cross-pollination and hybridization are difficult to prevent in plants with distinct male and female flowers (such as squashes and sweetcorn). The plant's flavour and appearance, as well as the quality of the seeds, can be influenced by cross-pollination.

Saving seeds from biennial plants (plants that take more than one season to produce seeds) like carrots or beetroots is difficult to do in small gardens or spaces as it's a pretty complicated process; you need to have a dedicated section of the garden for this plant, which will grow into flower, and they need to be kept in optimal conditions.

Make sure to save seeds from open pollinated varieties and not F1 varieties. Open pollinated varieties are often heirloom seeds that have been saved over the years and passed on from one generation to another. They maintain similar features of the previous crop but they also adapt to the climate conditions in which you are growing them. On the other hand, F1 varieties won't show any similar feature with their parent plants and they might also be infertile plants that don't produce true versions of the previous vegetables or flowers.

Always select the strongest-looking vegetables and fruit and avoid collecting your seeds from the weak or weird-looking ones. Ideally, you'd need fruit and vegetables with an even shape, bright colour, firm and not soft at the touch, no signs of pests or disease. You'll increase your chances of having healthy, highly productive plants by simply spending a bit of time looking out for these features.

SAVING TOMATO SEEDS

The ground temperature is usually too chilly for a ripe tomato to germinate when it falls to the ground naturally. The gelatine that surrounds the tomato seeds also lessens the likelihood of them sprouting right away. Warmer temperatures in the spring reawaken the seeds and cause them to germinate. This generally occurs when the gelatine that once surrounded the seed has vanished. Here is how to save seeds from a tomato:

1. Simply scoop the seeds and gelatine into a cup.
2. Cover the jar tightly with cling film and set aside for two to three days, depending on the temperature. To avoid mould, mix it twice a day, but don't worry if you get any; it won't hurt the seeds.
3. Your seeds should drop to the bottom after two to three days. Although most seeds sink to the bottom, a few kinds may float.
4. Drain and rinse your seeds before drying them on a paper plate. If you use kitchen paper, they will stick to the surface.
5. When they're entirely dry, put them in a paper bag and save them for the following season.

SAVING CHILLI SEEDS

The first step when saving chilli seeds is to leave them long enough on the plant until they wrinkle. Usually, I stop watering when the pods (chillies) are looking almost ready so the plant starts to focus all its energy into the development of the fruit.

1. Slice open a wrinkled chilli and remove the porous part surrounding the seeds called the placenta (most of the time this is white but it could be different colours).
2. Remove all the seeds and lay them on a paper plate well spread out, making sure they are not touching each other.

FUN FACT

The placenta is also the spiciest part of a chilli, contrary to the common belief that it's the seed containing the majority of the capsaicin (the compound that makes chillies spicy).

SAVING PEA AND BEAN SEEDS

You don't have to do anything other than wait for the pods to dry up and turn brown on the plant to save seeds. The roots of peas and beans, which are nitrogen-fixers, should be left in the ground after harvesting all the pods. To put it another way, they take in nitrogen from the air and store it in root nodules. Over time, the nodules in your soil will release nitrogen, which other plants can absorb. Ideally, you should cut peas and beans when young so the majority of this nitrogen stored in the roots is still available to be absorbed by other plants.

1. Before shelling the pods and separating each bean or pea, it's ideal to collect all of the dried pods and let them sit on a surface indoors for about one to two weeks.
2. Until you're ready to use them, you can store them in paper envelopes in a cold, dry place. For best results, soak the seeds overnight in water before using.

STORING SEEDS

Storing seeds properly is an essential step to keep them viable for a long time. I highly encourage you to buy paper envelopes as they are perfect to keep the seeds in the right conditions. Plastic could also work, but it's bad for the environment. If you use it, do not get the transparent bags, as seeds should be kept in total darkness.

I bought a photo case and clear craft folders, which come with 16 inner cases, and it helps me to organize all my seeds by category, sowing time or in any way I like. It was actually one of the best purchases in terms of seed organization. You could also make a spreadsheet on excel to update yearly with all your new varieties, saved seeds, quantities and any other detail that could make your life easier for the next season ahead. Keep them in an area with no humidity, at room temperature, being careful of temperature fluctuations and direct sunlight.

Storing seed box bought online (old cassette storage)

TRANSPLANTING PLANTS

Once seeds have sprouted in their indoor or covered trays, you will need to transfer them to the garden or growing space where they will thrive.

Preventing root shock is a primary concern when dealing with a plant (also known as transplant shock, which might stunt your plant by blocking, slowing or, in some extreme cases, killing the plant – see page 88). If you follow these simple procedures, your plant will quickly adapt to its new location.

The best time to transplant plants outdoors is early spring and autumn when plants are dormant. We've seen longer-lasting frost waves in recent seasons. As a rule of thumb, in spring I wait a few weeks after the final wave of frost is gone before planting. A quick online search for "last frost date" can provide the information you need.

A common practice is to transplant large plants as well as newly germinated seeds to allow the roots to expand and, as a result, the overall growth of the plant. Also, some plants, such as the bearded iris, need to be divided and replanted in order to flourish once more. Most plants that are cultivated in containers take up all of the available space with their roots and begin to mould themselves into the container shape as they mature. As a result, the roots can only grow so large and generate so much because there isn't enough space for them to spread out. Using a pot at least twice the size of the old one makes transplanting your plants from one container to another or onto open ground quick and uncomplicated. Not only does transplanting aid plant growth, but it also allows you to examine the roots, remove any diseased or decaying soil and then replant the roots in a new soil mix before the final transplant.

As a result of the improved nutrients provided by this new soil blend for plants, their overall health and wellbeing will improve significantly. If you have done a treatment like this, it is imperative that you take steps to reduce the symptoms of transplant shock. But if you do it right, transplanting can be a simple and inexpensive method to extend your garden space and improve the overall quality of your plants. Ideally, transplant as early in the day as possible, or as late in the day as possible, to minimize stress and shock to the plant.

In order for plants to adapt to a new environment, they must be moved gradually from an indoor environment to an outdoor one. To achieve this, take them out and put them back in each day for longer periods of time. Once they've been outside for a week or so, they'll be ready to take on the elements. When a plant is moved from an indoor environment (for example if you had plants started off indoors under artificial light) to an outdoor environment, this process is known as hardening off.

You can tell if your plant is ready to be moved by lifting it out of its pot and checking to see if any of its roots are showing from the bottom of the drainage holes. If this is the case, it indicates that the plant has filled the space and the roots are searching for new areas to develop.

HOW TO TRANSPLANT

Get everything you need ready before you begin transplanting your plants so you don't have to waste time running back and forth.

You will need:

- Water-resistant marker
- Pots
- Soil mix
- Tags

To minimize root damage, I usually make sure to thoroughly wet my plants before transplanting them. Don't remove the plant out of the pot by its stem unless you want to cause it harm. Instead gently squeeze around your container until the root mass slides out, or tip your container upside down, holding the soil with the stem of the plant in between your index and middle finger. As an alternative, you might use a butter knife to remove your plant from its seed cell. Charles Dowding seed cells have a bigger bottom hole so that you can just stick your finger in and remove the plant out of the seed cell. If you have more than one seedling in a container and you don't plan on planting them together using the multi-sowing approach, gently pull them apart. Using a bowl of water, soak the roots and gently pull them apart.

You may easily move plants by placing the old container inside the new one and making sure that both of its upper edges are equal in height before securing the new one to the old one. Get a new container, fill it with soil mix, then slide the old one out so you can plant your new one. The soil should be watered as soon as you plant seedlings in their new home so that the dirt around the roots is firmer. Firm soil is preferred by plants because it allows their roots to grow and develop into a strong rooting system.

Generally, it is recommended not to transplant your plants any deeper than the roots were already. However, I usually make a hole with a dibber or trowel that is slightly deeper than the actual size of the root mass of my plant. Simply make a hole and slide in your plant, gently applying pressure with your fingers so the root mass is in contact with the bottom of your hole. There's no need to fill the hole with extra soil. Simply water it as soon as you have transplanted so the roots can sit in a moist substrate, ideal for their growth. I do this so the plant is tucked into the soil, protected from wind or temperature drops during the night. However, there are a few exceptions, like tomatoes – they have stems that can develop roots and hence benefit from being planted deeper than other plants.

Roots coming out of the bottom of my peach tree

TRANSPLANT SHOCK

Plants can suffer from transplant shock if you make a mistake when transplanting them. Because of the stress it experiences after being moved, a plant is unable to thrive after being transplanted. Roots may not be able to adapt to a new environment because of a lack of water, or an insect infestation. The newly relocated plant may become dormant, stunted or die as a result of this stress.

Even though there is often no cure for transplant shock, there are a few therapies that may be able to rescue your plant. Even better, it's frequently possible to avoid it entirely.

Water retention may be an issue if you notice that a plant's leaves begin to wilt as soon as it's moved. This can be swiftly remedied by digging around the plant, breaking up the roots, and soaking, if the roots were not sufficiently broken up prior to transplant.

Other times, it indicates that the roots haven't fully taken hold in their new surroundings. To help the plant recover when suffering from shock, I spray top and bottom with aloe vera gel and water and I keep the plant in shade. Plants treated for a few days should bounce back and start growing.

To make your aloe vera gel mixture you can cut a few leaves of aloe (no need to remove the skin) and blend them with unchlorinated water until the mixture gets to a dense texture. Water the affected plant by mixing 250ml (1 cup) of the mix in 8–10 litres (2–2½ gallons) water. There's no need to remove the big bits of aloe left in the water.

Alternatively, you can make a spray mix by scooping out the gel from a few leaves, adding 250ml (1 cup) of gel into 8 litres (2 gallons) of unchlorinated water and filtering it with a fine mesh. Spray the top and bottom of every leaf, making sure to do this process either early morning or late in the afternoon, out of direct sunlight.

Another way to help the plant recover is to try trimming the plant back. This works because smaller plants focus more energy on root growth, as they do not have to expend energy growing leaves or stems.

ROOT BOUND

Most of the time you buy a plant in your local nursery or garden centre, they may look just fine but they are likely to be root bound to the pot. This means that their roots have developed pressed up against the sides of the container it has grown in, and the roots become tightly packed together.

Many people feel that a plant with many thick roots is better than one with few thin yet dense roots, but they are wrong. A root-bound plant may continue to generate its roots in a tight, circular arrangement after being transplanted into the garden, but these roots are rarely sent out into the surrounding soil. The plant would eventually become tangled up in its own roots and perish. A plant with a loose root ball and a lot of loose, bare soil around the roots is a preferable option.

To recognize a root-bound plant is pretty easy. The next time you are visiting your local garden centre, you could either lift the plant and check the drainage holes to see if many roots are poking out of the bottom, or it's perfectly fine to slide the plant out from the pot and check the root mass. To do this, simply tip the plant upside down by holding the stem in between your index and middle finger, gently squeeze around the pot and slide it off. Don't force it; you just need to check a few inches of the root mass to understand the overall condition of the plant.

If your only options are root-bound plants, or if you left a plant to grow in the same pot for too long, there are still options to get your plant back on the growing track. You can either break apart the root mass with your hand or with tools like a knife/trowel, or apply vertical slices along the sides and bottom of the root mass. This will encourage the plant to generate new roots not following the shape of the pot where they were bounded. Do not worry about breaking the root mass; the plant will form new roots. Also, a sign of healthy roots is a white colour and almost hairy appearance, so if you see brown roots, you are actually doing the plant a favour by trimming them off.

A root bound plant

GROWING VEGETABLES, FRUITS AND HERBS

CHOOSING WHAT TO GROW

Now for the fun part – choosing what to grow! If you're looking for a range of ideas that I highly recommend for beginner gardeners, turn to Part 4, where I share my top plants to start planting in any garden. However, here I will go over a few specific vegetables, fruits and herbs that I think are worth delving into a little deeper.

Opposite: August harvest from the backyard

GROWING MUSHROOMS

Growing your own mushrooms is an amazing way to maximize food production, especially if you own a small growing space like my urban garden in London. It is also an excellent way to help your plants thrive by improving their capabilities of water and nutrient absorption thanks to a few varieties of mushrooms, such as wine caps. I learnt most of the things I know about growing mushrooms from my dear friend Elliot from Urban Farm-It.

Many of you know me from the videos I upload onto the internet, but we aren't the only species to do this; plants have their own internet, too! It allows them to communicate with each other, even over very long distances at times. It's all thanks to fungi called mycorrhizae (see below); most existing plants have a mutual relationship, as the mycorrhizae acts almost like an extension to the plant's root systems.

Personally, I really think mushrooms are one of the most fascinating things to study. They are also considered to be the "meat of the vegan world" due to them being rich in proteins, vitamins and minerals.

If you can, I recommend making contact with a local mushroom farm as they will be able to offer you spent mushroom blocks that you could fruit straight from the bag or you could even crush it and grow some mushrooms from a bucket!

WHAT IS MYCELIUM?

I mentioned the word mycorrhizae, and I'm pretty sure you asked yourself what it means and what it has to do with a garden. Under the forest floor, a fascinating network of fungi is intertwined with the tree roots. When we think about fungus, we typically think of mushrooms sprouting from the ground. Fungi produce mushrooms, but the majority of the fungi live as a huge network of mycelium, or tiny "threads", entangled with the roots of trees. The tiny "threads" of a fungus, the mycelium, wrap or dig into tree roots. "Mycorrhizal networks" formed by mycelium connect individual plants and transfer water as well as nutrients and minerals between them. In the same way that a network of connections forms the internet, mycelium is like the forest network connecting all of the living things together.

This network allows trees in a healthy forest to exchange water and nutrients with each other. In dark areas, saplings' leaves don't get enough sunlight to perform effective photosynthesis, but mycorrhizal networks allow seedlings to obtain nutrients and sugar from older, higher plants. Research carried out at the University of Reading found that plants recognize the root tips of relatives and prefer to send carbon and nutrients through the fungus network to those relations.

The mycorrhizal network acts as a distribution system for the fungi's carbon supply and the health of trees connected by mycelium. About 30 per cent of the sugar produced by the connected trees during photosynthesis is held back by the mycorrhizal network as compensation for their services. Because the fungus feeds on the sugar, it can build up phosphorus and other minerals in its mycelium, which the trees can then use.

Tree–fungi networks cannot function without hub trees. The forest's "mother trees" are the older, more experienced trees. In most cases, they are the ones with the most ties to fungi. The young seedlings may now access deeper water sources since their roots have grown deeper into the ground. The mycorrhizal network is used by these hub trees to monitor the health of their neighbours and give them the nutrients they require.

As you can tell, the mycorrhizal network is important to the health and productivity of any plant in any part of the world. Using our motto of "Do as nature does", whatever we can do to establish and protect these fungal connections in the soil will benefit our gardens, as well as making us feel even more interconnected with the earth around us.

There are many different ways to grow mushrooms. Each offer different levels of affordability, difficulty, time and quantity of mushrooms produced.

GROWING MUSHROOMS INDOORS

First off, let's start with making a grow room in your own home. This will take a little more time to set up and won't be the cheapest option but it produces great results quickly. This doesn't need to be done in an entire room. It can be room-size or cupboard-size; that's up to you and down to what's available in your home. You will want it to be quite tall though to help with temperature control.

Once you have chosen where to set it up, you will need to line your growing space with reflective sheeting. This will keep light from escaping and also stop natural light from coming in, which will interfere with the environment you're trying to create for your mushrooms. A grow tent works great and can be bought fairly cheaply online.

I use a Spider Farmer SF1000 light system for my set up. They can be bought online and are quite expensive, but are worth it. They have a wide colour spectrum and a low output of energy so they are good for the environment while still working effectively. For holding up my lights I have added an adjustable ratchet roll system that allows me to calibrate the exact distance I need.

You can leave the light at the minimum setting of around 30–50cm (12–20in) distance from your mushrooms. For circulation and air extraction I use a carbon filter connected to an air extractor – the RVK Fan and Rhino Pro Filter Extraction Kit is perfect for this.

After you have set up your grow room you will need to prepare your mushrooms. I use a few varieties, but I recommend oyster mushrooms for your first attempt as they are the easiest and quickest to fruit. They grow quickly and are easy to look after without too many needs.

There are two options for mushroom kits if you are ordering online. The first option from Marvellous Mushrooms (www.marvellous-mushrooms.co.uk) will come as a hardwood sawdust block, which is pre-inoculated and fully colonized with a full set of instructions on how to set it up. The mycelium will have already grown all the way through it so it will be ready to produce mushrooms on arrival. Get your bag and cut the top off; if there is a lot of coral-like growth on the surface, then just remove that with your hands and set it aside to add to your compost. The kit comes with four skewers that you can add inside the bag at the four corners to support the outer bag cover.

With the kit you will also get an outer bag. Cut eight holes about 2.5cm (1in) wide in that bag, then spray the inside of it with water. Make sure you remove the outer bag once a day to let out the carbon dioxide and spray inside the bag a few times.

Alternatively, the second option from Urban Farm It (www.urban-farm-it.com) is a kit that comes disassembled. You will get a substrate, mushroom spawn as well as all the instructions. You just have to add boiling water to the bag with the substrate, let it cool down, drain the water and mix in your fresh spawn (seed). Store in a cool dark place and let the mycelium (roots) take over the substrate. Bring the kit into the light and keep it moist by spraying water over it.

Place the mushroom block inside your grow room and make it like autumnal conditions – between 17–19°C (62–66°F) with a 70 per cent humidity. There's no need to be absolutely precise about temperature and humidity, the mushrooms will still grow, but those are just indicative numbers for optimal growing conditions. Now wait – you'll see mushrooms begin to appear very quickly!

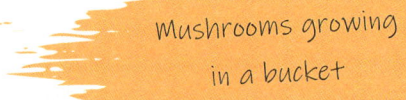
Mushrooms growing in a bucket

GROWING MUSHROOMS IN A RAISED BED

Growing mushrooms in a raised bed isn't only easy but can be very effective if done properly. All you need is a damp/moist area, some wood chips and mushroom spawn of your choice. For beginners, King Stropharia, also called wine cap, is highly recommended.

Firstly, you will want to find where you can set up or build a raised bed. It doesn't matter too much where you decide to build it, as long as you can fill it with wood chips and keep it from drying out too easily. Somewhere that is in the shade through most of the day is ideal but I have had raised beds in full sun which also worked; they just needed a constant and large amount of water throughout the day.

Once you have set up the bed, you will need to put a layer of cardboard on the base. You can do this without cardboard, but if you have lots of weeds growing it is recommended. I usually do this where I have plants growing already or where I'm planning to grow plants so I don't add the cardboard. However, the cardboard is good in case you don't plan to plant anything for the next month or so as it will help to keep in moisture and suppress any weeds in the soil below.

Create a layer of wood chippings or straw on top of the cardboard. I prefer to use straw, as wood chippings (especially if fresh) could potentially deprive the plants of nitrogen and you will have a slow growth and yellowing. Put a few handfuls of your mushroom spawn on the first layer of the straw, then add more straw. Repeat until you are satisfied with a thick layer of straw (2–4 layers). Use about 0.8kg (28oz) mushroom spawn per 1sq m (3sq ft) of your bed. The spawn will feed off the straw for a few months, then begin to produce mushrooms. As you add each layer, ensure the wood chippings/straw and mushroom spawn are evenly distributed across the bed.

Adding straw has quite a few benefits. However, I add straw as mulch only if I plan to grow mushrooms or for potatoes and strawberries. Otherwise, I use compost as mulch as it is much richer in nutrients and biodiversity of microorganisms. The straw will keep everything moist and stop it from drying out. It will also help to ensure any water that falls on the bed will stay trapped within there. During the colder months it will provide a bit of warmth and protect the spawn from the harsh winter cold. Once this is done, it will need a good soaking since a lot of moisture is needed to get things started. Continue watering over the coming months to avoid the bed drying out, as this will halt any mushroom growth!

If you weren't able to set your mushrooms up in a shady area or beneath the shelter of a tree, then it's best to add some shade netting above the bed. This will prevent the soil from drying out due to sun exposure but it is not a big issue if you live in a zone with a climate similar to the UK.

Maintaining your mushroom bed shouldn't be too difficult, provided you have easy access to water and a good memory! It will need a soak once a week, unless of course the rain has done that for you, over the colder months, and once or twice a day if the weather gets really hot. After four to six weeks you should see signs of life in the form of white filaments. And after about two to three months you should begin to see mushrooms on the surface.

 ## GROWING MUSHROOMS IN BUCKETS

Growing mushrooms in buckets is, of course, on a much smaller scale but the benefits of this are that it's easier to manage, costs less and it can be done if you don't have a garden or the space for a raised bed.

The mushrooms you can grow in buckets are different to mushrooms grown in beds though. This is due to the nature of how they grow. When growing in a bucket you will need to choose "side fruiting" mushrooms. These are the ones you will often see growing on the sides of trees. Starting with oyster mushrooms isn't a bad idea as they're very fast growing and less sensitive to growing conditions.

You can experiment with this idea however you like but I would suggest using a 20 litre (5 gallon) bucket as they give ample room for substrate and for lots of mushrooms to grow.

Mushroom substrate is a material that feeds the mushroom mycelium. It also provides the mushrooms with moisture, nutrients and energy. Different species of mushrooms prefer different substrates so it's important to do some research before you attempt to grow any. A good substrate is full of fibrous material, such as cellulose, lignin and hemicellulose. A substrate can be made from many different materials, as long as you research the best substrate for the mushrooms you're growing, you can't go wrong.

Once you have your substrate ready it will need to be pasteurized. This will make a nice, clean environment ready for the mycelium to take over and can simply be done by being placed in boiling water for one to two hours.

You will need about 10 per cent of the bucket to be filled with spawn, so for a 20 litre (5 gallon) bucket you'll need about 2kg (4.4 pounds).

You will need to prepare the bucket by drilling 1cm (½in) wide holes, about 12cm (5in) apart, all around the bucket. Lastly, tape up the holes from the outside with micropore tape. I manage to grow mushrooms without taping my buckets but if you want to be sure, it is best to use the tape. Now fill the bucket with a layer of substrate, then a layer of spawn, and keep repeating this until the bucket is full, making sure the last layer is your substrate. Clean your hands with a germicide soap and mix the substrate with your hands for a more even distribution.

Leave the bucket in a warm and dark place, around 20°C (68°F). Within two weeks the bucket should be ready and after three weeks you will start to see fruiting on the side of the bucket. Once this has happened, put the bucket somewhere light, but not in direct sunlight, with good airflow and a temperature of no less than 10°C (50°F).

Optimum time for harvesting oyster mushrooms is when the caps flatten, then begin to curl upwards. Harvest them as soon as you see this otherwise they will start to deteriorate.

GROWING MUSHROOMS ON LOGS

Growing mushrooms on logs is a very affordable method with plenty of options. Again, oyster mushrooms are a great choice to start with.

You will need to find the right log to grow your mushrooms on. Ensure you take logs from healthy-looking trees and avoid any that already have any pre-existing fungi, otherwise you might find yourself growing some unwanted (and potentially dangerous) mushrooms. They say you only eat the wrong mushroom once!

The logs will need to be at least 10–14 days old, as they might have fungicide property, impeding the mycelium to take over. The size of the log is very important too – smaller ones will produce mushrooms quicker but they will produce them for a shorter period of time so bear this in mind when you are finding your logs. A diameter of no more than 30cm (12in) and length of no more than 1.5m (5ft) is ideal – as long as you can easily transport it! Something you have to think about when you live in a city like London. You could get a few odd looks on the train or if you try to balance it on your bike.

Once you have found the perfect log(s), start drilling holes for the spawn. About 50 holes for a 1.5m (5ft) log is enough. Drill 1.5cm (¾in) deep holes along the length of the log. This depth will leave a small space on the inside of the log where plugs won't reach up to and this is where the mycelium will grow.

Begin the next row of holes about 5cm (2in) from the first line. Make sure the holes don't line up, but instead run in line with the middle of the distance between holes. When all of the holes are drilled this should create a diamond-like pattern.

Lightly hammer dowels into the holes. They should be just below the surface of the wood and enough to allow room for wax to be applied on top. This next step is very important as it's to prevent any damage being done or anything infecting the mycelium. Any wax will do, so long as it stays in place and it's not toxic.

After all of the plugs are waxed, the log is ready for incubation. They are best kept somewhere shady with high humidity and good air circulation. If this isn't an option for you, you can cover them with a cloth. If winter where you live is particularly cold, then store them inside your garage or a shed.

The logs will need a soaking once or twice a week. If they ever dry up, no mushrooms will grow! So it's very important.

Mushrooms that grow on logs will produce fruit once or twice a year for around four years, with spring and autumn being the most common times for this to happen. Harvest your mushrooms as soon as you can, as if you leave it too late they won't be as tasty and the texture will deteriorate.

Oyster mushrooms growing inside

Wine cap mushroom

GROWING TOMATOES

Tomatoes are one of the easiest plants to grow and care for; it doesn't matter if you are a beginner or an expert gardener. They are really tasty, too. Homegrown tomatoes taste so much better than your local store-bought ones and there are so many amazing varieties to choose from. Because of this, tomatoes are one of the most common vegetables to grow in gardens, however they require a solid structure for support to grow and provide a high yield.

Tomatoes are botanically defined as a fruit as they form from a flower and contain seeds. They are brilliant to have at hand as you can use them in so many ways either raw, or in cooking, from a delicious tomato salad to a spectacular spaghetti bolognese. What could be better than wandering out into your own garden and cooking with your very own homegrown tomatoes?

One of the most common classifications you will see on a label or packet of seeds will be determinate or indeterminate. These terms refer to the way a plant will grow and their natural tendencies.

DETERMINATE TOMATOES

Determinate tomatoes are varieties that grow to a fixed size and ripen all the fruit pretty much all at once in a short period of time. That is usually within a two-week period. Once all the fruit has ripened the plant will start to be visually less vigorous and have almost no new growth.

Determinate tomatoes are often referred to as "bush". They do not continue to extend in length and they tend to stay in a compact size. They are generally smaller plants than indeterminate varieties and tend to grow to 1–1.5m (4–5ft) tall.

Pruning and removing suckers from determinate varieties is generally not needed because they stop growing on their own. Despite their compact size, staking is always recommended. They will be supporting a heavy crop/load once all the fruit starts to ripen and grow in size. This will put a considerable amount of weight on the branches and they could snap.

Crushed heart tomato, determinate variety

INDETERMINATE TOMATOES

Chocolate lightning

Indeterminate varieties are tomato plants that continue to grow in length throughout the season. This is why you will sometimes see them referred to as "vining" tomatoes. Indeterminate varieties continue to set and ripen new fruit throughout the growing season until the frost kills the plants. They will give you a slow and steady supply of tomatoes rather than a single and large harvest. However, they will start maturing a bit late in the season because they will focus a lot of energy on the initial growth of the plant.

With indeterminate tomatoes, you will also have to pinch the side shoots called suckers in order to control the growth of the plant and keep it manageable. The majority of tomato varieties are indeterminate, including heirloom and cherry varieties.

Indeterminate varieties need large stakes or caging because of how long they grow. The plant could reach 2–3m (6–10ft) or taller and become really heavy. Both tomato varieties require staking in order to support their growth throughout the whole generative process and until the fruit is fully mature.

TRAINING TOMATOES

One of the main things I like to plan ahead of time is the support for my plants. You could potentially have the best seeds on the market, but without the appropriate care and a solid structure to support it, the plant's growth and yield would be minimal.

It is important to train your tomato vines, as they produce better when they are lifted off the ground. This is because there is less impact from pests and rot, allowing them to stay healthier and produce more. It also makes it much easier to pick them as you are bending your back less.

Last year I had most of my tomato plants inside the greenhouse and I used metal wire with bamboo sticks along a metal frame of the greenhouse to support them growing. However, this method is time consuming and pretty annoying once the plants were due to be removed from the greenhouse growing space.

You have a few choices for how to train them. You could tie your vines to a tall wooden stake. The downside of this is that the ties can slide down the stake, which can then strangle the vines. The tie can also snap from the weight that is put on them.

A lot of people choose to use cages of fence panels or concrete reinforcing wire mesh. I am not a huge fan of this as they create an almost impenetrable area hiding the ripest and sometimes tastiest fruit in the centre of the cage that are almost impossible to reach. You can also purchase wire "tomato cages" that are often quite flimsy and don't do the job you need them to.

A much better idea is to build a trellis.

DIY A-FRAME TOMATO TRELLIS

For my A-frame tomato trellis I used store-bought wood, but if you can find secondhand materials that you can repurpose and use, all the better. If you are planning to use any wood preservatives I would recommend you apply it first before starting to assemble your tomato trellis. You can make this trellis bigger or smaller; just adapt the measurements to suit your needs.

The wooden pieces I selected were 2.5 by 4cm (1 by 1½in) and I cut them in sections of 1.8m (72in) in length as I wanted to build the trellis pretty high to grow indeterminate varieties.

1. I started by building the sides of the structure, which are made by cutting two wooden legs with a hand saw with a top cut at 180 degrees (just for aesthetics).
2. Now that you have cut your wooden legs you can cut the braces. The first one will be 24cm (9½in) in length and you will place it 10cm (4in) from the top, and the second one will be 88cm (34¾in) and you will place it 15cm (6in) from the bottom. When fixing the wooden braces remember to place the screws off centre; this way you will lessen the chances of splitting the wood.
3. I used an electric drill to screw in 6cm (2⅓in) length screws. Now that you have got one of the sides ready you can proceed to create the second one.
4. When you are ready to put the two A-frames together, have someone hold up one of the A-frames and put a long trellis wooden bar on the top, going from one side to the other, fixing it with some screws. Repeat the same process with the other A-frame and you will have the base for your wooden trellis structure for your tomatoes.
5. To make it more stable I also fixed a long wooden trellis bar going from the bottom of one A-frame to the other one. You could skip this step, but I prefer to make it more solid. I kept a 88cm (34½in) gap between the two wooden legs at the bottom and 16cm (6½in) gap at the top. This is just based on sizes that I am using for my raised beds. You could also make it bigger or smaller.

6. The last step would be to run some hardy cotton twine or durable string from top to bottom which will be the main support for your plants. You will want to have as many lengths of twine as tomato plants you're planning on planting. You may also want to put some screws at the top and secure the string to make sure it doesn't move.

7. Building the trellis is really easy and doesn't require any power tools (except for my drill but I could have done it without it). You don't need any building background; you just need to follow these instructions and make sure you pay attention to the details.

8. If you build this correctly it will last you for a few years. All you need to do is cut off the wires and replace them with some new ones each year. If you use biodegradable materials you can also compost it. It's also really easy to dismantle and build again if you are moving.

YOU CAN MAKE A TRELLIS OUT OF ANYTHING!

There are lots of things you can use to make a trellis. Once, I even made a pea trellis out of an old bike wheel. I simply used an old half oak barrel, filled it with compost and drilled some holes all around it ready to put the twine though. Then I stuck an old broom handle in the drainage hole (you could use anything) and attached the old bike wheel to the top of it. I then attached jute rope through the holes and connected it to the wheel. I planted some peas, making sure I put the pea seedlings behind the rope. I watered them and attached them to the rope as they grew to make sure they were supported. It is amazing what you can use that is free or affordable to plant/support your plants in the garden.

Left: Zima tomatoes

Right: An A-frame trellis

HOW TO BUILD A TEEPEE

If you are planning on growing vines like tomatoes, peas or even squash, cucumber or marrow, then it's a great idea to build a teepee to support them. Not only do they look great, but they are easy to make and move about, and allow the crop to grow at a convenient height for harvest.

They are amazingly simple to build, and can be made from a variety of found material, from bamboo canes and branches to old guttering or even old rake or broom handles. The important thing is that you have at least four equal length poles about 1.8–2.4m (6–8ft) long.

It is also worth considering how long you want it to last for. If you are planning to grow annual veggies, like tomatoes, and don't mind rebuilding it every year or so, you don't need to worry so much about durability, however if you want a more permanent solution, then you might want to think about using a more sturdy material. Four decent branches from an old apple tree you or a neighbour has pruned would be ideal.

Whatever material you decide upon, putting them together is the same and ridiculously simple.

First, you will need to tie the tops of them together with good, strong garden twine or copper wire before spreading out the bottoms and digging them a couple of inches into the ground or pretty deep if you have a lot of wind. You can add further support around the bottom if you like, by simply planting the poles deeper.

If you are growing peas or cucumbers, the last step is attaching garden twine in equally spaced rows, about 15cm (6in) apart, going up the teepee. This is to give the vines something to attach to as they grow. Plant your veg around the outside of the teepee so that they cover it when they grow, meaning you have easy access to your crop when it comes to harvesting.

GROWING MICROGREENS

When I asked people on my social media accounts if they were growing microgreens, I received so many questions that it definitely deserves its own section in my book.

Microgreens are a huge variety of young vegetable greens that are about 2.5–7.5cm (1–3in) tall depending on the variety. They are packed with nutrients and come in many different varieties and flavours. They are absolutely perfect for livening up any dish and make great micro salads, too.

I started growing microgreens when I first came to London because every time I went to a restaurant I was served different dishes with a huge variety of microgreens on them. I fell in love with them instantly.

I have lived in many houses since I have been in London without a balcony or outside space. I thought about how to grow without much space and low light. Microgreens are one of the best things to grow no matter where you live. You just need some basic equipment and you are good to go.

Once you harvest your microgreens, you can compost the substrate as it's full of nutrients and roots, which will decompose nicely and turn into something valuable to reuse in your garden.

By growing a high amount of seeds in a small space they won't develop into full mature plants, but will be harvested when still small. Make sure that you don't buy your seeds from a random supplier (I buy mine from www.verdantrepublic.com, but there are many good sources out there). The usual scenario is that the average number of seeds per packet is really low and it won't be enough to completely saturate the surface of your tray. I use Biobizz light for my soil (www.biobizz.com), but there are also many different types, or you could use coco coir (also called coconut fibre).

Coco coir is a hydroponic growing medium made from coconut husks. This replaces soil by giving the plant something to grow in that supports its roots and keeps it aerated and moist. In nature, coconut husks not only protect the coconut from the sun and sea, but give it a great place to germinate that is free from fungus but rich in nutrients. Another great thing about it is that it is made from something that would otherwise go to waste, and is totally biodegradable.

GROWING MICROGREENS INDOORS

They are surprisingly easy to grow and once you start you will wonder why you haven't done so before. All you need is a shelf, a few grow lights and something to grow them in and you will be able to grow and harvest enough garnish for weeks, or even a month.

You will need:

- 250–500ml (1–2 cups) unchlorinated water
- 2 planting trays
- Light soil or coco coir
- Bulk microgreen seeds
- Grow lights (or sunlight)

1. Pour 250–500ml (1–2 cups) of unchlorinated water into the bottom of a planting tray. This means you won't need to water the surface of the tray too much. It also means the plants will absorb the water from the bottom, which can potentially mean they will avoid any fungal or bacteria infections.
2. Fill the tray with soil or coco coir. Leave a 2.5cm (1in) gap at the top of the tray, so that when you cut the base of your microgreens you won't end up taking any soil or dirt with you.
3. Flatten out the surface of the soil to make sure there are no bumps as you want to aim for a uniform growth of your seeds.
4. Sprinkle over the seeds, making sure there is an even spread. If you skip a few spots be sure to sprinkle some more so it is all equally covered.
5. Mist the seeds with some water to trigger the germination process. The exception to this is things like peas, which you need to soak in water before putting them on the soil to ensure a better germination rate. Check the packet instructions if you have bought your seeds, or a quick online search should tell you if it's needed or not.
6. Place the other empty planting tray on top of one of the filled trays. This will keep all the seeds under the soil level as well as ensuring a flat and even growing surface. Once the seeds start germinating, you will see the top tray lifting up. Plants are strong!
7. Leave the seeds for two to three days to see if they have germinated. Turn on the the grow lights and you will start to see the difference

(see Note below). Set a timer to regulate the lights. I normally set my timer for 16 hours a day but experiment with what works best for you. After another two days you will find some are already starting to get established.

8. Within two to three weeks of germination you should be able to start harvesting. You know that they are ready when you can see proper leaves appearing. Simply take a pair of scissors and snip them off just above the soil and, hey presto: you have microgreens!

Note: I put growing lights above microgreens when I grow them, but you don't need them at the beginning of the germination process or if you are positioning your trays in a sunny spot.

I use LED boards but there are many different types of lights that are great. The main differences are output power, energy and coverage (which means how many plants can be grown by the covering area of light). With microgreens you don't need to worry too much about the light that covers them, but that you keep the light as close as possible to the canopy. It is really important that you don't place the light too far away, otherwise you will end up with stretched plants. What we want is compact and small plants so that we can harvest really healthy microgreens.

DO I NEED TO BE AN ESTABLISHED GARDENER TO GROW MICROGREENS?

Growing microgreens is perfect for both beginners and established gardeners. You could even sell your microgreens! Why not get in touch with a few local restaurants or chefs and see if they want to buy them from you. People are always in need of microgreens as well as spices and aromatics.

PLANTING A HERB GARDEN

I really recommend growing your own herbs. They are one of the most expensive items from the supermarket but also one of the easiest things to grow. I have dedicated a raised bed to growing rosemary, oregano, two varieties of chives and thyme in my small garden. They will also grow well in pots, and most herbs survive throughout the winter and come back in spring. This will have a huge impact on your garden and your kitchen because of the amount of flavour you can get from a small area. The other great thing about herbs is that there are so many flavours to choose from that you would never find in a supermarket – from purple basil, which makes the most amazing pesto, to pineapple mint, which is brilliant in a cocktail.

I have made lots of mistakes along the way while growing, especially with mint. I am really glad I did so that you don't have to! Though making mistakes is of course how you learn. So don't worry; it is only going to help your understanding in the long run.

CHOOSING WHERE TO PLANT

The great thing about herbs is that you can grow them in areas where space is really limited, from a herb garden in a raised bed like I have done, in large containers, a hanging basket or even on your window sill in the kitchen. As long as it gets some sunlight it will be fine. You could even grow them in an old wine box.

The majority of herbs grow best in sheltered, sunny spots, so think about this when planning. Which part of your balcony or garden gets the most light? Don't worry if you only have a shady spot, though; you can still grow herbs.

WHICH HERBS TO CHOOSE

When deciding what herbs you are going to plant, make sure you think about what they need as individuals:

- What sunlight do they need?
- What moisture do they need?
- What type of soil are they happiest in?

Alternatively, herbs can, of course, be planted individually in their own containers – you will definitely need to do this with mint! Mint roots are called rhizomes, which means the mint creates an underground stem that produces new shoots and roots. If planted in open ground, mint will quickly take over your whole growing space, obstructing the growth of the other plants planted in the same area.

Also be sure to think about what herbs you like the best. There is no point growing coriander (cilantro) if you are someone that thinks it tastes like soap! Experiment with herbs and try new varieties. They don't need to take up much space and can really add flavour to your cooking. You can also dry and preserve them to be able to add value to recipes all year round.

Mediterranean herbs

Lots of perennial herbs such as rosemary, sage, oregano and thyme originate from the Mediterranean. They thrive when they are drenched in sun and in poor soil so you want to ensure wherever you grow them is well-drained.

Annual and biennial herbs

These are lighter herbs, such as basil, parsley and coriander, which need more moisture but can also thrive in part shade. If it is too hot, they will bolt, which means they will run to flower and seed. This will normally change the taste and make them more bitter. I sometimes let some of my basil bolt (going to flower) as a sacrifice to keep the beneficial insects happy, so it isn't all bad.

Herbs that love the shade

If you want to make sure you use every spot in your garden, there are lots of herbs that do surprisingly well in the shade, such as dill and parsley. Don't think you can't grow things in a shady spot on a balcony or shaded by other plants; this is a great way to fill the empty gaps in your garden with shade-loving plants.

Herbs that don't mix well

As mentioned previously, make sure you plant mint in a separate pot as otherwise it will take over. It happened to me once (see page 112). Lemon balm also likes to spread and take over, so grow it in a large pot on its own. Both will also spread to neighbouring pots after about a year, so be very careful where you position your pots.

WHERE TO GET YOUR HERBS

You can choose to grow them from seed, to clone other plants in your garden or from a friend's garden. You may even find wild rosemary and decide to clone it from a place you have visited so you can bring a lovely memory back to your garden. You can also buy them from a local nursery or grower or even use herbs from the supermarket.

CHOOSE YOUR CONTAINER

You could plant herbs in a raised bed (see page 42), use a terracotta pot or keep them separately on your window sill. What is important is that you want to be able to reach your herbs to harvest them. You also want to think about how they look. Some herbs will grow taller and are therefore better in the centre compared to chives that are better at the edges.

PLANT YOUR HERBS

Remember to think about what conditions your herbs like. Your mediterranean herbs need well-drained soil to thrive, and your annual herbs will want more moist conditions. I like to use a homemade compost to cover mine or you can use a good peat-free multipurpose compost from a local nursery or garden centre.

1. Make sure you have watered them first before planting them and remove any leaves that don't look great.
2. Gently split open the roots if they are tangled in the same shape of your pot and place them in the new pot or container. Make sure you are happy with how they look before planting them.
3. Label your plants so you remember what you are planting as I still do now. It doesn't matter how much of an expert you are, as there are new varieties coming up every year and it's hard to keep track with the amount of names.

Recycled hanging container herb garden

KEEPING YOUR HERB GARDEN ALIVE

Make sure you remember to water your herbs as they get used to their new home. Don't be scared to pick them and use them. Read up on the different herbs you are growing to find out more about them and discover new and exciting varieties to try.

I could write a whole book on herbs alone but I wanted to tell you a little bit more about my favourite basil and also mint, which was my nemesis in the garden, but I can confirm we are friends again now.

BASIL

This is a must to grow in my opinion. Basil is known to repel thrips, flies and mosquitoes, and acts as a protecting companion for planted tomatoes as it protects against these pests as well as milkweed bugs, hornworms and aphids. Basil also acts as a natural fungicide.

Basil is also known to improve the flavour of tomatoes as they share soil and space quite companionably. There is nothing better than cooking with tomato and basil in my opinion. Their combined scents go so well together; it is clear they are the ultimate couple. I add this plant to almost every raised bed or pot in my garden.

I also plant french marigolds with them, often the tangerine or African version. They have roots that communicate with the roots of tomatoes, creating a symbiotic relationship between the two plants. They repel harmful nematodes, which could be really dangerous for your tomatoes.

The tomatoes also help to protect the basil from getting sunburned. It acts like a very handy natural parasol.

Pruning

It is very important to top your basil plants to make sure they are really healthy. Many gardeners are shy about pruning their plants, but if you want a bushy, healthy basil plant that continues to produce tasty leaves you need to do this. It really pays to do this little and often and you can use the basil you.prune to cook with. Alternatively, you could preserve it by dehydrating it or making a delicious basil vinegar to go on a fresh tomato salad.

Pruning basil will help the plant grow better but you can also plant these tops and therefore maximize growth and production in your growing space. If you don't have room, why not swap basil for another herb with a friend?

What you don't want to do is just pluck off individual leaves and think: Yes, I am pruning this! This will not stimulate new growth. Get up close to your basil plant and look for the central stem. Cut this back to a lower set of leaves where two tiny leaf buds emerge from the leaf node. Cut this main stem about a 5mm (¼in) above the leaf buds. It is much easier to spot than you first think. If you are worried about getting it wrong, then watch my Instagram or Tiktok video to make sure you are familiar with where to cut and make your basil clones.

Now you have your cuttings ready to be cloned. What I do with a cutting like this is to simply remove all the lower leaves, and once the stem is exposed I fill a cup or jar with rain water or unchlorinated water (just leave your water in the open air for 48–72 hours or use any product like eco thrive to remove the chlorine from your water). Then stick your clone into the water and leave in a semi-shaded area. If you leave it in full sun you may risk it getting sunburned.

After 7–10 days lots of roots will appear out of the main stem. Once the roots are 2–3cm (¾–1¼in), you can then plant them in soil. In about a week, you should have a super healthy plant with pretty big leaves. You could potentially top it again already but I prefer to wait until it gets to a bigger size. It is entirely up to you how you'd like to shape your plants.

Basil Flowers

If you let basil plants flower, insects will go bananas to get to those delicious flowers. However humans won't as they become bitter to taste. This is one of the reasons why I always clone basil plants and make a few pots to spread around my garden and let them flower. It is worth sacrificing a few plants to get those companion insects, especially if you are growing tomatoes.

To stop your basil going to flower, pinch the flowers off as they go to seed. Don't chuck those flowers in your compost though. Take them into your kitchen – they are great in a pesto or, my personal favourite, on a freshly made pizza.

Left: Genovese basil

Right: Thai basil flowering

MINT

There are certain plants that are really easy to grow, but if you plant them straight into your garden they can take over the whole place, turning your dream garden into a real nightmare. Mint is one of them!

Mint is an aromatic herb. There is a great story behind this brilliant plant. Native to the eastern Mediterranean, mint gets its name from the nymph called Minthe. Persephone turned her into a lowly mint plant after she had an affair with Pluto (Hades).

The mint plant is very common and a favourite of many gardeners. It is pretty easy to grow your own. Mint tastes sweet and produces a lingering effect on the tongue. The fresh leaves have the most flavour and scent. I use them mostly to make tea or cocktails. You can store fresh mint in the fridge or you can hang it upside down until dry. Once dry, store it in a jar or a sealed plastic bag. This will allow you to enjoy mint all year round.

There are many different varieties of mint available and I am currently growing a few, including banana mint, chocolate mint, ginger mint, basil mint, lime mint, peppermint and, my absolute favourite, pineapple mint.

How to grow mint

Avoid growing different varieties of mint close together either in pots or in the ground, as you could potentially lose their individual flavours and different scents. A few years ago I made the mistake of planting mint straight in the ground in the only spot of open ground that I have in my garden. It took over the whole space, and trying to control it was absolutely pointless. I had to remove all the existing plants and dig up roughly 1m (3ft) deep of soil and sift through it. The reason is that mint roots spread easily because of the rhizomes. This means that even if a small bit of root is still in the ground it will develop new shoots. This is why you should always grow mint in isolation or in containers. It grows well in both full sun and partial shade. However, if you live in a hot climate it is recommended to grow it in partial shade.

Feed your mint with an organic fertilizer like well-rotted manure or a slow-release fertilizer such as insect frass or worm casting (see page 133). You should start feeding your mint when spring begins or roughly a month after you have planted it.

Water mint regularly and keep the soil moist but not soaking wet. A quick trick to understand if your plant needs water is to stick your finger into the soil and you can tell if it is dry or still moist.

Mint thrives in pretty much any kind of moist, well-draining, rich soil. I recommend buying a pre-mix from your local garden centre. Or you could potentially make your own. I make my own by mixing 50/50 good potting soil and mature compost.

You could also grow mint on your window sill by using well-draining soil and slow-release fertilizer. I also mulch the soil to retain moisture and limit the amount of weeds that could potentially grow in the same area where the mint is growing. Spread 5–7cm (2–3in) of mulch around the base of each mint plant.

Pests and diseases

I really don't recommend spraying any of your plants, including your mint plants, with any kind of pesticides. It could easily be ingested once you consume the mint. However, there are many kinds of pests that could potentially attack your mint. Mites and aphids are a really common issue for mint plants.

If you have a light infestation you could potentially just spray your plants with a strong jet of water and this will get rid of the aphids. As a last resort, insecticides might be needed. Look for insecticides with imidacloprid – this will kill the aphids without killing any other beneficial insects like bees and butterflies.

I also tried nematodes as a preventive measure or at the first sign of a light infestation. You could simply mix nematodes with water and directly water the base of the mint plant or spray the leaves. I personally noticed that two applications of nematodes one month apart drastically reduced the amount of pests attacking my plants. Natural predators like lacewings or ladybirds could be attracted or even released at the beginning of the season so you will have organic pest control in your garden; make sure to source native predators.

How to prune

Mint is a plant that grows really densely and sometimes in much larger quantities than we can consume. Don't worry even if you don't use it straight away, it is recommended to prune mint down and store it for later use. You should always prune back lateral shoots and chop off a few nodes. Your mint will benefit from pruning, especially at the end of the season when the plant is due to go dormant. I usually prune it down to pretty much ground level at the end of the season. Then the next season it will come back even stronger. This is also a great chance to clone your mint and make many more plants.

How to clone

To clone mint plants, you should simply cut one of the stems between three and six nodes, remove the lower leaves and stick the stem into a cup or glass of water. Depending on the weather you will have new roots within five to eight days and you can then transfer it into soil. Alternatively, you can plant it straight into soil and it will take root in 10–15 days. If you plant it in pots, don't plant it with any other plant or the roots will slowly suffocate all the other plants around it.

You can start harvesting mint leaves once it has multiple stems and they reach 15–20cm (6–8in) long. It will take about two months if you start it from seed or less if you bought plants from the nursery. Do not harvest more than ⅓ of the plant at any time as you could potentially weaken the plant and send it into its final decline.

Different varieties of mint

Native to the eastern Mediterranean, mint gets its name from the nymph called Minthe.

GROWING AN ORCHARD IN A SMALL SPACE

WHAT IS AN ORCHARD?

An orchard is a plantation of at least five trees or shrubs that have been intentionally grown and maintained primarily for food production. They can be made of one or many varieties of food-producing trees, usually fruit or nuts, but can also include sap, as in a maple orchard.

Dwarf fruit trees

Dwarf fruit trees are simply smaller versions of trees. They are easier to manage and maintain, especially in a smaller plot of land. They are created by grafting cuttings or shoots (known as a scion) onto the rootstock selected for its smaller size. Most dwarf trees will grow to about 2.5–3m (8-10 ft) tall and begin bearing fruit within three to five years. Although the yield won't be as high as a standard fruit tree, the fruit is of the same size and quality. The best part of growing dwarf varieties is that you can grow them in pots, and this is what I do in my garden! I use 30–40 litre (6½–9 gallon) pots for each dwarf tree, making sure to add enough nutrients and optimal drainage.

Semi-dwarf fruit trees

Semi-dwarf trees are somewhere between a dwarf tree and a standard-size tree. Where a normal fruit tree might grow as tall as 9m (30ft), the root stock selected when creating a semi-dwarf tree will limit its growth to about 4.5–6m (15–20ft). Again, these are easier to maintain than a standard tree and will have a significantly higher yield than a dwarf tree.

TAKING CARE OF FRUIT TREES

Location is of the utmost importance when it comes to planting an orchard. It is vital to map out the plot before you start planting or even selecting the fruit trees you wish to grow. Most fruit trees need a lot of sunshine, good drainage, at least 60cm (2ft) of slightly acidic (pH 6) sandy loam (loam is a term that describes a soil with a good, healthy mix of silt, sand and clay) and plenty of moisture. This is another reason why growing them in pots is brilliant and versatile as you can move them around your garden.

Another thing to think about is how low the ground temperature can go. If it frequently falls below zero, more delicate trees, such as citrus, will not survive and will need a conservatory or heated greenhouse to survive. Hardier trees, such as apples and pears, will survive the winter. However, a late spring frost could destroy blossom and decimate yield.

A sheltered, southwest-facing plot is ideal for most fruit trees as it will be exposed to the most sunlight and protected from the harshest weather. A walled or enclosed courtyard could work well, but "rain shadows" must be taken into account, especially if the tree is using the walls for support. The walls tend to dry out at the bottom, even in wet weather, so an irrigation system is vital.

Once you have selected a plot, it is time to select the trees. Choose the types of fruit that not only do you want to grow, but that are also more likely to thrive in the plot you have available. It might be your dream to have an orange grove in northeast England, but unfortunately the cold winters will almost certainly prohibit this.

The size of the plot will determine the size and number of trees that you can grow. Remember when selecting your trees that they will grow bigger and take up more space than when you first plant them. Try to avoid buying more mature trees as you are likely to inherit a myriad of problems. Instead, buy healthy 2–3-year-old trees. You might have to wait a year or two before your first crop, but at least they will come problem-free.

Traditionally, orchards are planted in a grid system, with rows of trees running north to south, maximizing exposure to the sun. This, however, is not essential, and the size and shape of your plot will determine your layout. On the other hand, sufficient spacing is essential and will ultimately be determined by the size of your trees once fully grown. Dwarf trees should be at least 3.5m (11ft) apart and semi-dwarf trees should be at least 5m (16ft). This will ensure sufficient exposure to sun and minimize root competition.

Trees should be planted when they are dormant, in winter or early spring. This gives the tree a chance to regrow the roots that have been pruned or lost in transplanting. If you haven't planted your orchard come the spring, the trees won't have a chance to grow roots and will find it difficult to establish themselves. It would be better to wait until winter when they go back to dormancy.

Once planted, new trees will require regular watering, depending on the weather. This will encourage root growth and give them a much better chance of establishing themselves. They also respond well to straw-based organic manure.

Any shrubs, grass or weeds that grow around the tree should be removed at least for the first three years, minimizing competition and allowing the tree to thrive. Keeping on top of this will also encourage you to visit the trees regularly.

Remember that your trees are living organisms, responsive to outside influences, including weather, climate and human interaction. By visiting your trees regularly you will build up an understanding of your tree's unique needs and behaviours, allowing you to respond quickly and appropriately should any problems arise.

ORCHARD ISSUES

If you have your orchard planted in good, well-drained soil, with plenty of sun and space enough for them to grow, growing fruit should be relatively straightforward, with few problems cropping up. That being said, even the most attentive gardener will come across something that troubles them from time to time, but with quick action most of these should be easily remedied with no lasting effect. The most common things that an orchard might face are poor drainage, frost, pests and disease.

Poor drainage can be potentially disastrous for most fruit trees. Stagnant water can cause the roots to rot, spreading to the inner bark and then throughout the tree. This means that the tree can no longer transport water and nutrients.

Symptoms of this are poor growth, discoloured leaves, defoliation (loss of leaves) and thinning of the crown (the very top of the tree). The best way to prevent this is to make sure that your substrate has plenty of sand and water and can drain away sufficiently. Check the orchard after heavy rain and ensure the water is running away.

The more hardy fruit trees, such as apples and pears, should manage with short, sharp snaps of frost while they are dormant in winter. For the more delicate trees, or in extended cold weather periods, you can buy horticultural fleece that you can use as a blanket to keep your trees warm. A late spring frost can also be protected against by using a fleece, but do be careful not to damage the delicate blossoms on the tree.

Do not spray your trees with chemical pesticides, even if creepy crawlies want to eat your lovely trees. However, it has often been said that there is no such thing as too many aphids, but too few ladybirds. If you do get an abundance of aphids, it is likely to soon be followed by an army of hungry ladybirds. Waiting for this to happen might be detrimental though, especially with young trees. Luckily, you can easily and cheaply buy boxes of live ladybirds to do the pest control work for you.

Other pests, such as caterpillars, slugs and beetles can be removed by hand, or, like the aphids and ladybirds, will naturally attract their own predators, therefore creating a biodiverse ecosystem.

Diseases, such as Apple Canker, Brown Rot and Grey Mould are rare, but if left unchecked could be potentially lethal to the plant. By removing fallen leaves and fruit you are reducing the risk of these from infecting the plant in the first place. Should they appear, simply pruning away the infected area should remove the problem and allow air to circulate.

 ## HOW TO TRANSPLANT TREES

Planning is key when it comes to transplanting your fruit trees. Be sure you know exactly where you intend to plant each tree prior to transplanting – it's not a good idea to dig your tree up and then leave it sitting out while you decide on its location. Make sure you have your substrate ready and pre-dig all your holes before planting. Fill the holes with water the day before to maximize moisture levels (this will also tell you if there is sufficient drainage).

The best time to transplant your trees is early spring, after the main frost, and before it stops being dormant. Prune the tree prior to transplanting to minimize loss of water and encourage new growth. Pruning before you transplant also means that the tree will be more manageable.

Dig out the tree from its original position, being careful not to damage the root ball and prevent transplant shock. That being said, there is a balance between the size of the root and how easy it is to move. If it is a large root ball you might want to trim it back in order to make it more manageable. Do so carefully, taking into account the two most important roots: the tap root and the feeder roots.

The tap root goes down directly under the tree and is mostly concerned with water. It is the main battery of the tree and so should be severed with care. Cutting too close can cause irreversible damage. If you are not sure, watch a few videos online to really understand what the different roots look like and ask questions. We all learn from others and people are always happy to pass on their knowledge.

The feeder roots, the ones closer to the surface that are more concerned with finding nutrients, are delicate. It is important to carefully keep as many of these as possible.

Use a sharp spade at an angle so you are digging under the tree, about 50cm (20in) from the trunk. This should cut cleanly through the root system, leaving enough for the tree to re-establish itself. Thick roots might need a couple of goes to cut through; try and do this as cleanly as possible.

Once you have dug all the way around the tree, give it a good wiggle to see if it is still anchored to the ground. If it is, push the tree to one side and use your spade to cut through the roots.

Now it's time to lift the tree – do so carefully, trying not to damage the roots or disturb too much top soil. It's a good idea to lift the tree directly to the equipment you plan on moving the tree with. This could be anything from a tarp, a wheelbarrow or even the back of a truck. Remember, trees can be heavy, so you want to do as little lifting as possible. You can always ask a friend or neighbour to help you, with the promise of some of the produce as a thank you when the tree produces a lovely harvest for you. It is a great way to connect with others through nature.

Once you have moved the tree to its new position, make sure that the hole is the right depth for the tree. You might want to either dig more or fill the hole a bit so that the trunk sits at the same ground level as before. Make sure that the hole is damp, but not waterlogged, and orientate the tree to your preferred position. Remember that once it is dug in, you'll have quite a job repositioning it. So it is important to get it right now – it will also reduce the physical labour involved.

Once the tree is in the hole and in the correct orientation, you can cover the roots with a good-quality compost and gently firm down. A good watering can of seaweed solution will reduce the chance of root shock before gently trampling down with your feet. A heap of good-quality mulch piled over the base of the tree is a good idea to protect the roots, prevent weed growth and lock in moisture. Have a look at my chapters on how to make a good mulch to help with this (see page 165).

Staking a tree isn't usually necessary, and can even be damaging to it. Not only could you damage the roots, but staked trees tend to put their effort into growing tall trunks, rather than thick ones, which can be detrimental later on. If the tree is planted in a particularly windy area, or the ground soil is shallow, it could be beneficial to stake the tree by planting two stakes, one on each side, at the edge of the hole you dug and attaching them to the tree with strong twine. This will minimize damage to the tree and allow it to sway in the wind, encouraging a wide trunk.

Once transplanted the tree should be watered well and regularly to give it the best possible chance of survival. You could use a DIY watering system to help with this (see page 165) as it will reduce the effort needed and water wastage.

 ## HOW TO PRUNE

Pruning a tree can be quite daunting to the uninitiated. It needn't be though – with a little guidance, it can be a relatively simple and very satisfying task. Your aim when pruning a tree is to take off old, unproductive wood and allow for new growth. You will also create space in the centre of the tree that allows light and air to flow freely throughout the tree. The light will enable the growth to take place and the fruit to ripen, and the air will help prevent disease.

Before you start pruning your tree it is important that you are prepared. You will need a sharp pair of pruning shears and a pruning or bow saw. Blunt tools not only leave jagged, untidy edges, but are potentially dangerous. Like using a blunt knife in the kitchen, it is more likely to slip and cut you and leave a more jagged cut, which takes longer to heal.

If your tree is large then you may need a ladder. It is advisable to have a sturdy A-frame or tripod ladder, as propping it up against a branch you are about to cut off could end in disaster. I have seen this happen before so it is a good idea to double check!

Trees should be pruned in their dormant stage, when the leaves have fallen away and before they bud. In the UK, this is usually between December and March, but can vary depending on location and tree type.

As a rule of thumb, between 10–20 per cent should be removed, and this should be done evenly across the tree. Avoid giving your tree a haircut by just pruning the top of the tree, or you'll end up with all the new growth going upwards. This won't produce fruit and you will end up just pruning it every year. It will take up space in your garden or urban space without giving the yield you have hoped for.

Firstly, take off the suckers and water sprouts. Suckers are long shoots that grow from the base of the trunk or roots, basically a new tree growing from the old one. As the name implies, they suck up all the energy, diverting it away from fruit growth. Water sprouts are similar, but come from branches that have suffered damage or stress. Both of these should be removed with shears as close to the tree as possible.

If any disease has taken hold in the tree, pruning away the affected areas should prevent it from spreading and encourage healthy regrowth. Dead, dying or broken branches can be removed for the same reason. Take these off below the damage or disease, where the wood is healthy, preferably just above a spur (the knobbly bit that leaf, fruit or shoot buds grow out of).

Next, take off any crossed or inward-growing branches. This will train the tree to grow in the right direction, maximizing light and airflow. These should be taken off as close to the trunk or primary branches (the ones that give it structure, sometimes called scaffold branches) as you can.

If the branches are too thick for shears, use a saw. Make a cut on the underside of the branch about one-third of the way through, then cut down, on the outside of the undercut, angled toward it. The branch should come off easily under its own weight.

Reduce the previous year's growth by cutting the primary branches close to spurs that face the way you want them to. This will thin out the tree and promote the growth that you want.

Laterals or side branches are basically the twigs that grow from the branches, and these are where most of the fruit is grown. These should be left where possible, unless the area is overcrowded or they are too long (over 15cm/6in), in which case use shears and choose to keep the ones that face outward.

Finally, take a step back and consider the following points:

- Does the tree look even?
- Are the branches growing in the direction you want them to?
- Is there enough light and air getting to all parts of the tree?

If the answer is no to any of these questions, continue pruning. If you answer yes to all three, you can save and use the pruned branches for your raised beds (see page 46).

All you have to do now is wait for the tree to produce fruit and look forward to enjoying them. You can choose to share and eat them freshly, or you can preserve them and keep them to use throughout the year. You could even make an apple pie mix and freeze it so you have it to hand for those cold winter days where you want something comforting to warm you up after a few hours in the garden.

Left:
Pruning borders
in the backyard

Right:
Peach on a
semi-dwarf tree

SUCCESSION SOWING

I always want to make sure I have optimal output in my garden and nothing goes to waste. While I cook, preserve and share with friends and neighbours, I also try to avoid too many gluts by succession sowing where possible. It also means that I don't have to quickly pick a lot of produce in a short period, which takes a lot of stress out of harvest time.

By planning my garden I can make sure that I plant seeds in small batches in succession, so I have access to fresh crops throughout the growing season, rather than planting them all at once and having a huge glut.

It is important to work out what type of crop you are planting, how long it takes to grow and the length of time they produce fruit or veg for. It's also worth thinking about how perishable a crop is, and how likely you are to eat or preserve it.

Vegetables that mature quickly, such as carrots and spinach, are ideal for succession sowing. By planting them at regular intervals, in small batches, you will find that you have a continuous, manageable supply of fresh veg.

It's a good idea to mix up the varieties of veg that you are growing so that you have some quick-maturing plants, and some that take a little longer, and perhaps last longer in the ground. Not only will this stop you from getting bored of the same things all the time, but you will ensure that there is always something to pick throughout the season.

With plants that mature quickly and are prone to bolting, such as coriander (cilantro), succession sowing is great for providing a steady crop.

Plants that produce crops over a long period of time, such as tomatoes, crops that store well, such as onions, or ones that need a long time to mature, like leeks, don't need to be successionally sown.

As a rule of thumb, I start sowing seeds outdoors in mid spring and a bit earlier indoors. Then, on average, I will plant again every two weeks. In spring this might be as far apart as three, or even four, weeks depending on the plant. Come summer this might be every week. Again, it's very important to plan, but also be flexible depending on the weather and what your crops are doing. Keep an eye on what your other plants are doing, and plant your next batch when they start to become more developed.

There is always an element of chance as weather and climate conditions have a massive effect on the rate at which plants grow. A sudden sunny spell might mean that a crop planted recently comes to maturity at the same time as one planted a while ago, causing a glut. Not necessarily a terrible problem, though, as you'll have lots of lovely food to give to friends and family.

Chicken of the woods mushroom
with fresh garden salad

"Make your garden a
community affair and invite
neighbours or friends and
family over for dinner in
your outside space."

Swedey crunchy rolls

COMPOSTING METHODS

WHAT IS COMPOST?

When I started gardening, one of the first things that helped me reduce my carbon footprint and get more passionate about growing food was composting.

Methane, a powerful greenhouse gas, is produced in landfills by organic waste. Methane emissions are greatly decreased when food waste and other organics are composted rather than going into landfill.

Compost is nothing more than a mixture of organic matter, which gets decomposed by worms, fungi and microorganisms. In my garden, I like to call it black gold!

You could either create a compost bin that sits on open ground or you can keep it on concrete by raising it from the floor like I did in my garden. Worms will find their way in, no matter where it sits! For my first compost bin, I recycled an old bin, drilled holes at the bottom for drainage and all around for aeration, and used it to make my own compost for many years until I changed it for a bioreactor, which I'll explain in the next section (see page 128).

A compost aerator

MAKING YOUR OWN COMPOST

To make your own compost, there's no right or wrong way of doing it; by adding materials rich in nitrogen (green materials) and carbon (brown materials) you'll have compost! See the box on the next page for examples of what is meant by green and brown materials and other items you should never use in your compost bin. If you have enough space to create a compost pile with a big volume, the compost will produce heat, but if you have a small pile like mine, it won't heat up as much. Either way, it will work and serve you well in your garden!

As a rule of thumb, I add 5cm (2in) of brown materials any time I have some and a sprinkle of green materials. Doing this in layers will help to keep the structure of the compost pile. Start doing this from scratch and within about six to ten months you will have a nice compost. The ideal ratio of carbon (brown) to nitrogen (green) would be 30:1. Too much carbon and the pile will not heat up enough so the decomposition would drastically slow down. Too much nitrogen and the compost pile will start to smell bad and be very moist.

It's not only about having the right ratio of materials. There also needs to be enough moisture and oxygen for thermophilic bacteria and fungi to start thriving and decomposing the materials. To check the right amount of moisture, simply grab a handful of compost, squeeze it and check if you have a couple of drops coming out. To make sure you have enough oxygen, you need to turn your compost pile or add chimneys. I started using a tool called an aerator, which works incredibly well and is really cheap to purchase (see picture on page 124).

The beauty of composting is that you are turning waste into something valuable that can be used as a soil improver, mulch and a growing medium. I used to think that things affected by diseases like blight, powdery mildew or even weeds could not go into a compost pile, as is commonly taught. However, after chatting with Charles Dowding (see page 20) and learning his highly efficient method for composting, I started adding all these things into my compost pile. It is safe, because diseases such as blight need living material to thrive on, which they won't find in the compost, and weeds have a limited amount of energy – once you take them out of the ground they simply run out of energy and die. This happens when you start a hot composting pile to produce your own compost.

In my garden I even had cold composting piles, which you don't even need to turn, but just leave undisturbed to decompose. However, they have a few differences in the final result, as, in my opinion, cold composting is not as good as hot composting when we collect the final compost.

WHEN TO USE IT

You can use your compost to start a no-dig garden from scratch. It's a one-off investment, as it will stay fertile for many years. I mostly use it to top up all my raised beds and pots once a year by spreading 2.5cm (1in) of compost at the end of the season and without adding anything extra. However, you need to make sure to add the right materials to get a good organic compost that is a valuable addition to the soil.

EXAMPLES OF GREEN AND BROWN MATERIALS

There's a lot of confusion about greens and browns in compost piles. For example, coffee grounds are brown in colour but they are as green as grass clippings or vegetable scraps in terms of composting due to the high amount of nitrogen they contain. When we talk about composting, you should always refer to nitrogen and carbon. Nitrogen-rich materials are basically anything that is fresh and usually moist, with a high water content (for example, food waste). Carbon-rich materials help to absorb moisture and balance the pH of your compost pile but also provide a source of food for fungi and hold some spaces for air, which is essential in hot composting.

Green materials:	Brown materials:	Materials not to use:
fresh manure	dry leaves	dairy
weeds	shredded paper	fats
leaves and roots	cardboard	oils
coffee grounds	straw	meat
tea bags	wood chips	bones
grass clippings	tissues	dog or cat waste
food scraps	wood ashes	black walnuts
garden waste	fruit waste	plants treated with
hay		pesticides

 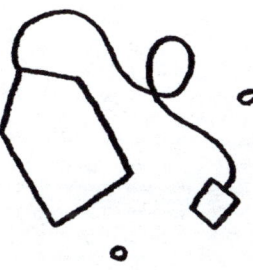   

MAKING YOUR OWN BIOREACTOR COMPOST BIN

At the beginning of 2022 I met an incredibly knowledgeable person named Michael Kennard, founder of the Compost Club. He runs an amazing project on a mission to create a community of composters to reduce the carbon emission of food waste and divert it from landfill or incineration. He has been a gardening enthusiast since his late teens and took a keen interest in composting when he got his allotment in Brighton back in 2016. Since the COVID-19 lockdown of March 2020, Michael took a deep dive into soil microbiology and established a business intercepting food waste from the conventional waste stream, instead creating a biodiverse compost with a broad spectrum of beneficial biology.

He helped me to create an incredible composting system in my garden called a bioreactor, which could work in pretty much any space by adapting the volume. Building this composting system is a great way to create biologically diverse compost relatively quickly. You would need a few cheap materials if you'd like to build it yourself.

You will need:

- Pallet
- Steel mesh
- Cable ties
- Staple gun
- Wood chips (see page 129)
- Tarpaulin
- Some rope or bungee
- A pipe to fill around, or something to push down with for the chimneys

Bioreactor composting system by Michael Kennard

1. Lay the pallet on the ground and attach wire mesh to it. Ideally this mesh will have about 1cm (½in) holes to stop too much compost escaping.
2. Make an upright hoop of the mesh to sit on the pallet like a cylinder and fasten the ends together with wire or clips.
3. Fill this with a base layer of wood chippings or something high in carbon about 2.5–5cm (1–2in) thick.
4. Add your composting materials. Some people recommend a lasagne style with layers of each ingredient, but Michael says that mixing them together gives quicker and better results.

HOW TO SOURCE WOOD CHIPPINGS

Sourcing wood chippings can be quite tricky, especially if you live in a city like London. However, there are a few tricks to get some for your garden or compost pile. There are a lot of tree trimmings happening all around us, especially in urban areas, by arborists, tree trimming companies and even electric utilities. Back in the days they used to make bonfires to get rid of them, but since that stopped happening they all make big piles of wood chippings, which need to be disposed of.

It is likely you will be able to find such a company that is easily accessible to make it easy for wood chippings to be delivered to you. Contact your local council and ask for the contact number of these companies or keep an eye on parks and local woodlands and ask them in person. If you need just a couple of bags for your garden, bring some bags with you and, in most cases, they won't mind sparing some. Alternatively, team up with your neighbours and share big deliveries of wood chippings with them.

BOKASHI – MAKING COMPOST WITHOUT A GARDEN

Without an outside area, you can still create your own compost and give it away to friends with gardens or simply minimize your waste by recycling your food scraps, even without a balcony.

You can't go wrong with Bokashi. Bokashi is a Japanese word that means "fermented organic matter". It was invented by Dr. Teuro Higa, a professor from Okinawa, Japan, in 1982. For generations, farmers in Asian countries, including Korea, have intentionally collected and cultivated soil microorganisms. They believe that by using this method the amount of inorganic soil amendments will be reduced.

Basically, almost any grain could be used as a host to be inoculated with Bokashi. You just need to use a brew that attracts the right bacterial strains. The brew will get inoculated with beneficial microbes that thrive in an anaerobic and acidic environment. (Anaerobic in plain English means oxygen-free.) The grains will be submerged in this brew and left to ferment along with molasses or brown sugar, which provides the nutrients for the microorganisms to thrive. The inoculated host is then dried and packaged for long-term storage after the fermentation process is complete. When water comes into touch with the bacteria, they will become active again and revive.

Yeasts, lactic acid-producing bacteria and purple non-sulphur bacteria make up the majority of the microorganisms.

Bokashi is made in a variety of ways, but this is the fundamental technique.

 ## HOW TO MAKE BOKASHI

Bokashi really is useful because, despite anyone's best efforts, there is always a small amount of food waste that comes from cooking, so having a way of composting it in your kitchen is a fantastic idea.

You might worry that having compost indoors will be smelly or messy, but from my experience that is not the case. I keep my Bokashi bin in the kitchen, and there is absolutely no smell. It's really good to just chuck in food scraps after you finish cooking.

A commercial Bokashi bucket is the best method to use for your food waste. This 2.2kg (5lb) plastic bin is well sealed at the top and has a spigot at the bottom. (The fluids need to be drained every now and then and this spigot makes this process easy.)

With Bokashi, unlike traditional outdoor compost heaps, you can add all of your kitchen leftovers, including meat, dairy and oils, excluding a few things like large bones or already mouldy food. The bacteria will take care of the waste disposal process.

For this reason, avoid adding anything to your Bokashi bucket that has already begun to decompose or has mould on it, as these bacteria may be able to outcompete those in your Bokashi.

There is a layer of grains at the bottom, followed by a layer of food trash. To remove any air pockets, a second layer of grains can be sprinkled on top. You should sprinkle some Bokashi over the food waste you're stacking and then push the compost down to get rid of any air bubbles after each layer is added, and keep stacking food waste.

After a few days, you'll notice a small amount of liquid at the bottom of the bin, which you can use in your garden at a ratio of 500:1. Make sure to use the liquid within a few days. For me, the liquid has little practical application outside of that, so I just pour it directly into the drains to keep algae and bad odour at bay.

At least three weeks after it's completely full, you can seal the bucket and leave it to ferment.

For the first month or so, the Bokashi pre-compost, like the anaerobic compost produced by digesters, is quite acidic.

Before planting, make sure the "pre-compost" has a week or two to integrate into the soil before allowing plant roots to touch it. Some people feed their vermicomposting worms with Bokashi material and they do just fine, but I have not tried this process before.

The pre-compost from Bokashi can be added to regular compost piles to speed up the decomposition process. If you decide to add your fermented food scraps directly into your soil, Bokashi should not be planted for at least two weeks after it has been buried in the soil. By burying it in a compost pile, this can be avoided because it finishes decomposing there. Additionally, it tackles the problem of finding unused space in small gardens and speeding up decomposition in your compost bin or pile. I don't have to sacrifice any room in my limited growing area because of this.

It's perfectly fine to give it away to relatives and friends if you don't have the space to use it in your garden, but it's still great to reduce the amount of waste produced by your household.

HOW TO MAKE YOUR BOKASHI GRAINS

You can make your own Bokashi grains by mixing EM-1 liquid (Effective microorganisms), molasses and a grain or grass-like substrate. Once made as instructed below, you can either use it as it is or spread it on a tray away from direct sunlight to dry off, then store in a bag in a cool dry place.

You will need:

- 15ml (1 tablespoon) molasses
- 250ml (1 cup) warm water
- 1 tablespoon of EM-1 (you can find it online in many organic stores)
- 500g (1lb 2oz) wheat bran

1. Mix the molasses and warm water together, and then add the EM-1.
2. Add the wheat bran and mix together until the bran feels moist but not soggy.
3. Transfer the mixture to an airtight container (a white bucket works well), seal and leave it in a warm, dark place for two to three weeks. Make sure you don't open the container during this time or the process won't work!
4. After two to three weeks the bran should smell fermented. Any signs of white mould on the surface is a good indicator that the process worked.
5. The grains will remain usable for up to a year.

WORM CASTING

Vermicastings, or worm castings, are a type of organic fertilizer made by worms and used as a soil amendment. The goal is to create a better environment for the roots of your plants and this is when a soil amendment comes into play. It could be any material added to a soil to improve its physical properties, such as water retention, permeability, water infiltration, drainage, aeration and structure. Simply put, worm casting is worms' faeces.

Eisenia fetida, or "red wigglers", are the most often used worms for composting.

Organic food waste, garden trimmings and the bedding that the worms consume in the worm bin produce an ideal soil enricher. To be honest, I personally think there is nothing better than using this as compost in your garden!

The nutrients in worm castings are concentrated and highly accessible because of the ingredients that the worms were given. Worm castings, unlike other animal manures, are quite mellow and won't "burn" your plants, despite their high concentration of nutrients.

A mucous membrane forms on the castings during the process of passing through them, which means that these castings are transformed into ideal slow-release fertilizer granules.

As the raw material goes through the worm's body, beneficial microorganisms and bacteria are also introduced.

Incorporating worm castings into your garden soil improves the aeration of the soil, the drainage of water and the retention of water. As well as improving plant nutrient intake, worm castings also help seed germination.

Using worms to bioremediate or regenerate polluted soil reduces heavy metals, which is very impressive. Regenerating land is an amazing process involving the power of plants' photosynthesis to sequester carbon, improving soil structure, increasing the amount of organic matter and the microorganisms' activity.

HOW TO MAKE A WORM FARM

One of the most effective ways to turn kitchen garbage and food scraps into fertilizer is through a worm farm. You can set up a worm farm in the tiniest of locations, such as on a balcony or patio, and it requires minimal time and work to keep it going.

Worm composting systems, or worm farms, are in fact vermicomposting systems, and red wigglers (*eisenia fetida*), a species of worms, are one of the fastest composters. Make sure to not use normal earthworms that you find in your garden as they won't eat the food scraps quick enough.

Top left: Eisenia fetida ("red wiggler worms")

Bottom right: Worm farm found in the street, cleaned and works great

DIY WORM BIN

I learned how to make my own worm bin through following @Deannacat on Instagram, and I'm very glad I did. Deanna's website (www.homesteadandchill.com) has an excellent tutorial that walks you through the process step by step. There are a variety of ways to set up a worm farm, but I've always used a storage container with a lid until recently when I added a worm tower that I got from a friend.

A few things to bear in mind:

- Make sure the plastic you use is opaque so that worms can't see out. I bought a standard clear container and painted the outer part to avoid light infiltration. There should be no holes in the top of the lid to allow water to get in.
- Different containers can be used to make worm bins, as long as it doesn't have any holes.
- Air holes can be drilled into the worm bin's sides and near its top with a quarter-inch drill bit. The bottom of the worm bin should be completely sealed.

WORM BIN DRAINAGE

Drainage is a common query from novices when they first start building. If you cut holes in the bottom of the container, the worms will be able to get out. It's also not required to drain the bin as long as you keep the wetness and homogeneity of the contents in check.

Drainage catchment is included in some pre-assembled worm systems, such as the worm bin I recently acquired from my neighbours who no longer use it. Compost tea and worm tea are two different things, and what drains from the bin is not one of them. As it turns out, this is called leachate, and is formed when the worm bin is overly damp, causing it to leak. Besides being nasty, leachate doesn't have the beneficial biological activity found in real compost tea.

I usually check my worm bin by sticking one of my fingers into the substrate so I can tell if it's moist but not soaked wet and I also lift the bin to feel the weight. It might sound tricky, but as a rule of thumb lift the bin once you make it and refer to that weight any time you go and check it. After a few times you'll learn to identify any moisture issue.

WHAT "BEDDING" TO USE

You must first fill your bin with "bedding" before you can put any food waste in it. Rehydrated coco coir, sand and shredded newspapers can be used to make this bedding. Other good bedding can be made from shredded or cut-up cardboard, old phone books, straw and more. Standard bleached paper should be avoided at all costs.

The worms' digestive systems depend on the dirt for grit. Potting soil, which contains beneficial microbes, would be an excellent addition to your worm compost pile.

The bedding is your "brown" carbon supply in any composting system (see page 127).

Adding bedding is the first step to getting a worm bin up and running. When the bedding decomposes and is replaced by the worms (who devour it), you'll have to add more.

Worms prefer "brown" food scraps when they are fed scraps from established bins (carbon, view page 8). This is partly offset by the higher nitrogen and moisture content of the "green" materials, such as food leftovers or garden waste.

Make sure that your worm bin doesn't smell or look terrible by keeping it in good health. The most typical causes of a stinky bin and a poor habitat for your worms are an abundance of food, an absence of brown matter and an excess of wetness.

WHAT WORMS TO USE

The next thing you need are worms, which are both necessary and entertaining. For this, you'll need a supply of compost worms. Red wigglers, or *eisenia fetida*, are the most common. If you are based in the UK, I usually order mine from Yorkshire Worms (www.yorkshire-worms.co.uk) and they work perfectly.

To begin, you'll need a certain number of worms, which is determined by the size of your bin. I recommend starting with 500–1,000 worms for a storage bin of roughly 50–75-litre (13–20-gallon) capacity. You might begin with 1,000–2,000 for larger bins.

Your population will continue to expand as they reproduce. A worm population may more than double in 90 days in the right environment. Do not worry about having too many worms, since they will keep their own population in check.

WORM FACTS

- Worms are hermaphrodites, with five hearts and a lifespan of up to 13 years.
- Each worm can eat their weight in food scraps every single day!
- Also, another interesting thing that you will constantly find in a healthy and active garden are worm eggs! They look like small yellow round balls and can contain up to 20–25 worms, which will improve the worm population.

WHERE TO KEEP YOUR WORM BIN

These are a few rules and advice on the best place to situate your worm bin:

- The ideal temperature range for red wigglers is 12–23°C (53–73°F). Temperatures outside of this range will cause the worms to feed and reproduce more slowly, and extreme temperatures can kill them.
- Avoid placing your bin in direct sunlight. You know your worms are chilled if they form a writhing mass. Too much heat will make them try to get away.
- Avoid any areas where there is a risk of the bin getting wet. Worms can only breathe if their skin is moist. You want your worm bin to be damp to the touch, similar to a damp sponge. No leaking, no standing water and no entirely dry areas.
- Choose an area that is well-ventilated but not directly exposed to strong winds to avoid your worm composting system from drying up.
- Place your bin on top of cement or bricks to allow air to flow beneath it.

When it comes to your worm colony's health and stability, location matters more than any other factor. If you rarely go to the basement or garage, don't place your bins there because they won't last long. If your trash containers are correctly maintained, you won't notice any smells. If there's a problem, your nose will let you know, so keeping your bins in a spot you frequently visit is a bonus.

WORM-CASTING TEA

If you have a garden or land that has been used intensively using conventional practices but you are trying to transition to organic gardening, one of the best things to use along with IMO (see pages 142–3) is worm casting tea or compost tea.

This nutrient-rich brew is full of beneficial microorganisms, which will improve the quality of your soil food web. You can do this by using not only worm casting but almost any other form of compost brewed following this method. Don't worry if a few worms are still in the casting (including eggs) as they survive the brewing. To brew your tea, you will use aerobic conditions by introducing air into the bucket. Worms actually breathe through their skin, which means they will use the oxygen introduced in the bucket to survive.

There are many benefits involved when using compost tea in your garden, such as improving the moisture retention of your soil, less need to use any other kind of fertilizer, plants will be more resistant to pests and disease and much more. However, most people confuse the liquid draining from the bottom of their worm bin as compost tea but in reality that is called leachate, which is actually anaerobic and could mean harmful bacteria develops instead – the opposite of what you want.

There's no need to dilute the brew once it's made; you can go ahead and use it as it is. The worm casting tea can be used all over the garden, watering around trees or any plant growing in your garden. It is best to apply the tea after you have watered your garden so you will have less run-off of nutrients and ideal conditions for your microorganisms to thrive and multiply.

You will need:
- 0.5–1.25 litre (2–5 cups) of worm casting
- A brewing bag (either made from cheesecloth or use a reusable vegetable bag, or even a clean sock!)
- 85g/3oz/⅓ cup nutrient food – molasses, seaweed or humid acid (easily sourced online)
- An air pump (see Notes on the next page)
- Bucket
- 22 litres (6 gallons) unchlorinated or filtered water (see Notes on next page)

WHAT TO PLANT AND HOW

1. Add worm casting to your brewing bag and add 80ml (⅓ cup) of whatever source of nutrients you decided to use.
2. Insert your air pump inside a bucket filled with the water and turn it on so it will start bubbling and aerate the solution.
3. Submerge your brewing bag and leave it to brew for 12–48 hours. Keep the bucket in a shaded area, away from extreme heat and cold. Ideally, I do this in the kitchen as it produces minimal disturbance.
4. Once it finishes brewing, remove the bag and use the remaining solids left in the bag around your garden or add it to your compost.
5. Make sure to use your compost tea almost immediately or it will start degrading and become less effective (it will be at its best up to one to two hours after you finish brewing).

Notes:

- You can find many different air pumps online. I bought mine at a local store and it lasted for a few years. Air pumps generally come with a stone, which you should either replace each time you brew compost tea or clean thoroughly after every use. I prefer to use flat air stones as the air distribution is more even.
- To make unchlorinated water, simply fill a container with tap water and leave it to sit uncovered in direct sunlight for about 48–72 hours.

Worm-casting tea, and some worms!

NATURAL FARMING

HOW MICROORGANISMS CAN BENEFIT YOUR GARDEN

Microorganisms act as workers in your garden, providing essential nutrients to your plants. It is vital not to exclude good or bad bacteria from your soil's microorganisms when enriching it. As a result, your plants will be more resistant to disease and pests than those found in nature.

This concept is comparable to the concepts of yin and yang, the opposing forces of ancient Chinese philosophy. According to the dualistic idea, forces in nature that appear to be in opposition are actually complementary and interdependent. Another way of saying it is that both positive and negative forces must be present in order for them to produce each other.

It is possible to gather these complementary and interdependent microorganisms, known as Indigenous Microorganisms (IMO), in a variety of ways and in a variety of locations in and around the area where you cultivate your own food.

Using the microorganisms that have thrived and survived in your area works best because they are already familiar with the growing circumstances in your environment. They are significantly more powerful and effective than germs that have been created in a foreign environment and cultivated there.

Gathering and using IMOs is an important part of Korean Natural Farming, as they feed the soil, and the soil feeds your plants, rather than using non-natural, mass-produced fertilizers full of chemicals.

MAKING IMO-1

The best way to collect microorganisms is to look around where you live and find an area with high vegetation and similar growing conditions to your garden. It could be your local forest, hills or, if you are based in a city like myself, it could be a park. Wherever you choose, the location does need to be from a surrounding area rather than from your garden in order to introduce new microorganisms.

This may sound strange at first, but the best substrate that can be used to collect IMOs is steamed rice. The microorganisms are as picky as we humans are, so the rice should not be over-cooked or too al dente!

You will need:
- A wooden or cardboard box
- Kitchen towel
- Undercooked brown rice (enough to cover the bottom of the box with a thick layer)
- Paper or chicken wire (anything that can be loose and breathable as a lid)

Stage 1 – preparing the collection box:

1. First, prepare your collection box. This can be a wooden or cardboard box. Add a layer or two of kitchen towel at the bottom.
2. Add a layer of undercooked brown rice on top of that. Do not stuff the box with more than 5–7cm (2–3in) of rice or there won't be enough room for air to circulate. Also, do not compress it but leave it kind of loose. Without a sufficient supply of air you'll collect mostly anaerobic bacteria, and what you are after is a diversity including aerobic and anaerobic.
3. Cover the box with some paper, a loose, breathable cover or chicken wire. You could use another box upside down to protect your collection.

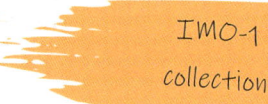

IMO-1 collection

Stage 2 – collecting the IMO-1:

4. Choose an area to start your collection – it should be somewhere with lots of vegetation. For example, this could be under a big tree or wherever you see mycelium already present on the soil. To spot mycelium you just need to look for the white cover that sometimes appears over soil (it reminds me of a ball of cotton).
5. Uncover the soil by removing the first layer of dry leaves or branches.
6. Position your collection box in this area. A small tip if you are doing it in a city park or local woods is to hide your collection box with branches and leaves to avoid it being discovered and removed; most people, if they do spot it, will think that it's a sort of trap for animals.
7. The moisture content of the rice in the collection box will attract indigenous microorganisms living in the local soil. The time this takes will depend on the weather conditions. At around 20°C (68°F) it should take about five to six days. If the temperature is between 30–35°C (86–97°F) it will take two to three days. Avoid doing it in the winter if you can. I'm on my fourth or fifth collection now, and I did it mostly during the cold UK weather and I'd say, on average, it takes around 10 days to have a nice collection.
8. After 3–10 days you'll have a covering of white fluff growing all over the rice. Don't worry if you see a few different colours appearing; as mentioned before, we are looking for diversity in both good and bad microorganisms so all microbes present will be useful.
9. Carefully remove the kitchen towel covered with rice and white fluff (this is the IMO-1) and transfer it to a bag or jar to be transported home and used in the next step of the process.

Notes:
- Wash the rice in water before using it for your collection, and remember to keep the cooking water, as it could be used for other things in your garden.
- Don't leave your collection box out for too long or it will start to degrade and turn completely into black mould, which is not recommended to use.
- Remember, with these processes you are interacting with bacteria so please wash your hands regularly and take all necessary hygiene precautions.

MAKING IMO-2

Once you have collected your rice that has been covered with IMO-1 (see previous page), it should look like a single block, or lots of small blocks, of rice stuck together by white fluff and a few different colours. This means your microorganisms are all active. What you need to do now is to put them into a state of dormancy for later use.

The basic process is to mix unprocessed sugar with the IMO-1 at a rate of 1:1. For example I weighed my rice and it turned out to be 200g (7oz) so I used the same amount of sugar. Don't worry if you add a bit too much sugar; it won't harm the mixture. However, if you add too little, the microorganisms will still be active and won't go into dormancy. The sugar pulls the liquid out of the rice so that the microorganisms dry out. This forces them to go into a state of dormancy, which is ideal for long shelf life. Once they come into contact with water when you're ready to use them, they will wake up and reactivate.

You will need:
- IMO-1 (see previous page)
- Unprocessed sugar (jaggery or demerara/turbinado work best; white sugar is not recommended)
- A glass jar
- Organic vinegar, for wiping
- Kitchen towel and a wristband

IMO-2

WHAT TO PLANT AND HOW

1. Mix the IMO-1 with the sugar. Don't worry if you see some sort of powder coming up in the air while mixing, it's just fungal spores, which are the seeds of good fungus.
2. Once it's all mixed well, you can transfer to a glass jar to store your mixture. Always leave some space in your container so that there is some oxygen present. As a rule of thumb, always fill your container to three-quarters full.
3. Gently compress the top layer of sugar, taking care not to pack it down too much. Another trick that I learned is to add an extra layer of sugar that acts like a cap for the mixture.
4. Always make sure that the top of your container is completely clean otherwise bugs will be attracted and eventually get inside the container. I always clean the rim of the jar with organic vinegar as it won't alter the fermentation process.
5. Close the jar by placing a layer of breathable fabric on top (such as muslin or kitchen towel) and sealing it with a wristband. Store it in a cool, dark area, such as a kitchen cupboard. Remember to clean the outer and upper part of your jar with organic vinegar.
6. If the mixture starts to bubble, just add some extra sugar. There's no need to mix.
7. You have now created your IMO-2, which you can use to enrich the soil in your garden with microorganisms. You have a unique, shelf-stable biology, ready to be used!

NOTES:
- If you find any insects during this process, do not kill them! Most likely they are woodlice and they are great for your garden.
- I always label my collection with the date and location so I can track what I use and where I collect my microorganisms.
- Remember, with these processes you are interacting with bacteria so please wash your hands regularly and take all necessary hygiene precautions.

HOW TO USE IMOS IN YOUR GARDEN

IMOs help to establish a healthy microbial balance on plant surfaces and within the soil, which is critical for nutrient delivery and disease resistance, making plants stronger and more resistant to pests. Even if there's nothing growing in your garden, it's still good to apply this mixture. I usually do this throughout the winter to get ready for the season ahead.

It is recommended to use the IMO solution at a ratio of 1:100, so the exact amounts you use will depend on how much IMO-2 you have. There's no need to be precise about the quantity. Just remember that there are no chemicals involved, so it can't harm your garden.

You will need:

- 1 tablespoon of IMO-2 (see previous page)
- 1 litre (35fl oz) rain water or uncholorinated water
- Mesh, for straining
- 10-litre (2½-gallon) bucket

1. In a large container, mix the IMO-2 with the water and stir well.
2. Drain the liquid through a mesh into a 10-litre (2-gallon) bucket.
3. You can now use it to water your garden as a soil drench or foliar spray. If you spray your plants, make sure to spray the upper and lower part of the leaves for an even distribution.
4. Repeat the process once a week to make sure the microorganisms are going deep into your soil and start to multiply, which will in turn improve the quality of your soil.

OTHER WAYS TO USE IMO SOLUTION

- IMO solution can also be added to compost for a microbial boost, or used mixed with other natural farming inputs as organic fertilizer.
- Adding IMO to your nutrient solution can also help to break down nutrients into a more bioavailable form for your plants to use. In simpler words, nutrients get broken down and transformed into a solution that is much easier for plants to absorb and process.

MAKING YOUR OWN NATURAL FERTILIZER

In my opinion, things have got out of hand when it comes to organic farming. Rather than appreciating what is readily available and inexpensive, many organic growers believe they need to purchase expensive items from afar.

There's a missing link with nature and we have lost the ancient techniques of nurturing food in line with nature, utilizing what's available in the nearby area where you grow your food in the most basic and cost-effective manner possible. Instead, farmers and gardeners are encouraged to turn to "experts" who claim that their products must be used for the best possible organic quality. But these products simply aren't necessary.

The principles of Jadam and Korean Natural Farming (see page 22) not only save money that would be wasted on these products, but they also reinvigorate growers' creativity. Because of the numerous macro- and micro-nutrients that are mentioned by companies promoting conventional farming, growing has become overly complicated. Fertilizer confidence is undermined as it becomes something that only specialists can advise on. But that is not true.

"We must be the masters of agriculture, once more in harmony with nature and take back food sovereignty!"

JADAM LIQUID FERTILISER (JLF)

There are times when Jadam Liquid Fertilizer (JLF) can be useful. Following Jadam's advice, I went to my local woods to get some plant material because I didn't have any crop residue (leftover plant material from my garden).

Using something commonly found in a city and often viewed simply as a nuisance, such as nettles, is ideal. Nettles thrive in organic matter-rich soils, which is why they grow near human settlements like London. Through my own research I discovered that nettles are high in enzymes and contain other plant growth-promoting properties, so I was convinced that they would be beneficial to my plants as they approach the vegetative stage. Nettles also happen to be an excellent aphid repellent, therefore I'll gladly use it in my garden.

I gathered all of the fresh growth of nettles I could find, stuffing them into a bag. (Always wear gloves when handling nettles to avoid being stung multiple times, which is an unpleasant experience! Alternatively, pick them from the base of the stem so you avoid getting stung.) While you are collecting, you will also want to grab some leaf mould (I explain how to do this on page 154).

You can make your own leaf mould in a variety of ways, including simply putting dry leaves in a garbage bag and punching holes in the bag for air movement. However, it takes more than a year to have a rich and biodiverse leaf mould suitable for this process.

Next, you'll need to add rain water or filtered water. (I use unchlorinated tap water as a backup if I don't have rain water.) Fill a bucket halfway with water, then add the nettles and leaf mould and secure the bucket loosely with a lid.

Leave the bucket for seven days before using. What is created inside is called Jadam Liquid Fertilizer, and it can be used like a normal fertilizer but has made use of something that would be considered a weed!

To use:

Dilute the contents at a 1:1,000 to 1:1,500 ratio, although this ratio should be lowered if you've had the bucket developing for a long time, like a year or so, because it becomes more concentrated over time. I use 1 tablespoon of Jadam Liquid Fertilizer per 5 litres (1 gallon) of water when spraying with a sprayer. Don't worry if you can't use it all at once. JLF gets better with time.

This liquid fertilizer will last an indefinite amount of time if you keep topping it up with more plant material and leaf mould. To keep the plant debris at the bottom of your bucket from clumping up, swirl it every now and again. Place the bucket in the same spot where you produce your crops because the microorganisms in the combination will develop and adapt to the same growing circumstances as your crops.

The beauty of this method is that you can use any plant material (as long as it isn't harmful) and get a fantastic source of nutrient-rich fertilizer. A mature tomato plant, for example, contains all of the elements required for the development of tomatoes, thus if used in JLF, it will be ideal as a fertilizer for tomato plants.

Top: Comfrey harvested in the morning
Middle: Nettles and brown sugar
Bottom: Jadam Liquid Fertiliser

The beauty of this method is that you can use any plant material (as long as it isn't harmful) and get a fantastic source of nutrient-rich fertilizer.

FERMENTED PLANT JUICE

I've been in love with fermentation since I was a kid; it is a fantastic process used to preserve vegetables and create delicious beverages full of probiotics. Since I discovered natural farming, I found fermentation methods worked for growing my own food, too.

Fermented Plant Juice (FPJ) is an easy, low cost and shelf-stable mineral amendment for your garden. By making this extraction, you'll be taking advantage of the weeds in your backyard that are in fact mineral accumulators, such as dandelions or nettles. The great thing about FPJ is that it contains enzymes, proteins, hormones and much more, all in a form that plants can absorb with minimal processing.

You will need to use brown sugar or demerara/turbinado sugar to make the FPJ and will need to ferment your plant material for about seven days.

Due to its high sugar content, brown sugar aids in the fermentation process by drawing liquids from the plant material and providing food for the bacteria involved. Fermentation yields a weak alcohol, which is used to extract chlorophyll and other plant constituents. To be clear, I do not advocate that you consume this juice in any way, shape or form.

HOW TO GATHER YOUR MATERIALS

The need for fast-growing plants is the most significant consideration when selecting plants for creating FPJ. This is because the faster the shoots that are used to create the juice grow, the more helpful compounds they will contain.

To me, spring is the ideal time of year to gather plant materials for creating FPJ. The new plant shoots are the most tolerant to temperature changes during spring and contain the most nutrients for rapid growth, making them ideal for creating FPJ. Although most people recommend collecting the plants when they are in full bloom in the summer. I highly discourage making this liquid during autumn or winter due to the scarce amount of plants growing (depending on where you are based).

Since I started adopting Korean Natural Farming, I've been continuously discovering local materials that I can use in my garden. I usually go out early in the morning to collect all the top shoots of these plants in the local forest when they are covered in morning dew. During the day, plants transpire a lot of moisture and photosynthesis takes place, which moves the plant energy throughout the entire body. You also want to avoid harvesting plants for FPJ after or during a rainstorm as it could wash away some of the microorganisms on the plant. Ideally, you should wait two days after the rain has stopped before collecting. Ideally, you want to collect 5–7cm (2–3in) of the plant leaves, and the top leaves are the best.

Once picked, rather than washing these plant leaves, simply wipe or lightly flick off any dirt or debris that may have accumulated on them. If you wash them, the lactic acid-producing bacteria and yeasts on the surface will be reduced, resulting in inefficient fermentation and/or insufficient yields of plant juice.

According to Korean Natural Farming (see page 22), 1cm sq of the leaf's surface includes 100,000 to 150,000 cells of microorganisms, most of which are lactic acid and yeast producers.

WHERE TO FIND MATERIALS

Korean Natural Farming strongly emphasizes using what is available to you in your local area. If you're unsure about a plant's safety, ask a forager for help identifying it. To identify wild plants, I have tried using a variety of apps, but they were not always accurate, so asking an expert is best.

Clover, dandelions, nettles and comfrey are all very common in the UK, where I live, and excellent for making FPJ. Alternatively, angelica, bamboo shoots, mugwort and seaweed are also known to create very good FPJ. But really you can use any plant that grows quickly, can withstand temperature changes and isn't poisonous or harmful to your environment.

Nettles have a high nitrogen content and many useful nutrients and enzymes for your plants. This makes them great to use as FPJ during the vegetative phase of almost any plants (when the plant is growing, so they need a lot of nitrogen).

I also usually gather clovers, which are high in nitrogen and can withstand rapid weather fluctuations. Because they are a nitrogen-fixer like the beans I mentioned before (see page 23), you can use them as a cover crop in your garden as well. A cover crop means seeds planted at high density and used to accumulate and store carbon, protect the soil and retain moisture.

Comfrey is one of my favourite plants to use in my garden, and due to its deep taproot and large root system, it pulls its nutrients from way down in the soil where most other plants can't reach. Comfrey's formidable roots mean it is high in just about every nutrient a plant needs, including the big three – nitrogen, phosphorus and potassium – and many trace elements.

In fact, I grow comfrey in a section of the garden and harvest it for the sole purpose of extracting the nutrients from this plant.

HOW TO MAKE FPJ

1. Cut the materials you have collected into 5–7cm (2–3in) pieces, especially if you are using fruit or large leaves; this increases the surface area for the brown sugar mixture.

2. For wet materials, weigh the plant materials and then weigh out the same amount of jaggery, organic brown sugar or demerara (this is a 50:50 ratio). Alternatively, if you are using something a bit more dry, you can start by adding three parts plant material and two parts organic brown sugar. Do not use processed sugar; the microbial activity is negatively impacted by white sugar.

3. Mix both materials in a big pan or bucket. To increase the osmotic process and pull out the plant fluids, coat as much of the plant material as possible with sugar. I usually spend some time making sure it is mixed and coated thoroughly.

4. Fill a glass container to the brim with the mixture of plant material and brown sugar. Metal jars will react with the solution, so avoid using them. Eliminate pockets of air by pressing the mixture down with your hands or a weight.

5. Clean the outer part of the jar and the rim with organic vinegar before closing it. You don't want to attract any nasty insects to your fermentation storage. Use a breathable material to cover the container. You could use muslin, a heavy cheesecloth or a towel for this purpose.

6. Position the container out of direct sunlight, in a well-ventilated environment that isn't too hot or cold (20°C/70°F would be perfect). The juice should not be refrigerated.

7. After 24 hours, the volume of the plant and sugar mixture should settle to three-quarters of the container. This is necessary for the fermentation process to proceed. The bacteria will not be able to properly ferment if the container is overly full. After the first 24 hours, you should check to see how the plant material has settled. Remove some of the plant material if yours is looking too full. Likewise, add in some more of the plant and sugar mixture if it doesn't look full enough, to avoid mould growth.

8. Fermentation will have begun when the mixture begins to bubble. This could take anywhere from five to seven days, depending on the weather and humidity, to complete the procedure.

9. Using a colander or sieve, remove the plant material from the fermented liquid after three to seven days. Let the mixture drain for several hours and do not squeeze or force it in any way. Let gravity do the job. I usually take notes on the liquid that I manage to extract from each different plant for future reference.

10. Do not throw away the solids – I usually add them back to the same jar, cover with water and a breathable cover. After roughly six months, you will have a mother forming which is really similar to the SCOBY (Symbiotic Culture Of Bacteria and Yeast) found in Kombucha. Strain the solids and you can use the liquid as cleaning vinegar for your future extractions of FPJ.

11. Store your FPJ in a cool, dark environment, in a jar with a permeable lid and always label your container with the date it was made and the plant material. It should keep for 6–12 months.

HOW TO USE FPJ

Applying FPJ to your growing space is really simple. There will be a strong smell of alcohol in the FPJ after it's made. Don't worry, this is how it should smell and is purely due to the breakdown of chlorophyll, which is exactly what we are after.

This is an incredible product to learn how to make and use but also to experiment with on your plants. As previously mentioned, it contains nutrients and many beneficial things in a plant-available form, which means the plant has to make a minimal effort to absorb them and process them.

FPJ is applied to the soil or directly onto plants by diluting it with water. A small amount of this solution could be used to cover a really big area of your garden. You should always start by diluting it at 1:1,000 or 1:500 with rain water or filtered water. Basically:

- 1 tablespoon FPJ to 16 litres (4 gallons) water is a dilution of 1:1,000.
- 2 tablespoons FPJ to 16 litres (4 gallons) water is a dilution of 1:500.

Apply this solution once a week or when your plant needs some extra minerals to recover from stress (transplanting, temperature fluctuations, etc.). You could also use this mixture to encourage seed germination. Simply dilute it using the same ratio and soak the seeds in the dilution for just a few minutes. In this way, all the nutrients and minerals necessary for the plant to grow will be available as soon as the plant pokes through the seed shell.

LEAF MOULD

While it's best to make FPJ in the spring and summer (see page 150), autumn and winter are ideal times to use leaf mould to protect and improve your garden's soil flora. Leaf mould is a far superior soil additive than compost when it comes to improving soil texture and microorganisms' activity. Water retention is improved, soil structure is improved, and soil micro- and macro-organisms, such as worms and bacteria, thrive in this environment.

The food chain is just as real in the invisible world as it is in the one we live in. Microbes are tiny organisms that can only be seen under a microscope.

Also, leaf mould is totally free and easy to obtain! Leaves that have fallen to the ground are broken down by fungi into a layer on the forest floor known as leaf mould.

Fungi adore leaves because they can store up to 80 per cent of the nutrients that a tree takes up through photosynthesis. Almost all of these nutrients are recycled back into the tree when the leaves fall off. However, lignin is still present in the leaf. Lignin acts as a buffer when mineral reserves fluctuate, allowing it to hold soil nutrients in excess. Lignin-rich leaves, on the other hand, disintegrate more slowly. In order to find leaf mould, it's preferable to keep an eye out for lignin-rich trees (see below).

HOW TO COLLECT LEAF MOULD

Leaf mould is so easy to collect and store. You can store it in breathable bags in your garden until you need it. You just need to find an area with high vegetation close to your house where trees have been dropping leaves. Move the first layer of leaves and collect the dark brown substrate underneath. (Before collection, please view recommendations explained in JLF section, page 148).

Don't be greedy and take too much from a single area; instead try to take small bits from different places. It's a gift from Mother Nature, so always be respectful and mindful about the life of the ecosystem.

Leaves can be divided into two categories: those that break down quickly and those that take longer to decompose.

In roughly a year, leaves with high nitrogen content but low lignin content will create good leaf mould. Oak, Elm, Ash, Birch, Poplar, Lime, Willow, Cherry and Beech are all included in this group.

Leaves with high lignin levels, on the other hand, will take longer to decay and become leaf mould. Hawthorn, Maple, Sycamore, Horse Chestnut, Deciduous Shrubs and Magnolia have leaves that break down slowly. The right balance of lignin-rich and lignin-poor leaves is ideal, but too much of either should be avoided. If you're unsure, start with less and add more later if you need to.

Certain leaves can really harm plants because of their acidity, so it's best to avoid them at all times. Don't be alarmed; they can be included if they only make up a small portion of the mould, although leaving them out is better. It's best to stay away from things like Acacia, Walnut, Camphor, Eucalyptus, Juniper and Pittosporum.

HOW TO USE LEAF MOULD

There are various ways to use leaf mould on your garden once you've collected it! Using leaf mould in your garden depends on how old the leaf mould is and we can distinguish it in two categories.

1. "Young leaf mould" – a mix of dark brown leaves, sticks and dark soil – I would usually add this to my compost pile to improve the compost biology.
2. "Well-rotted leaf mould" – when leaves begin to break up and crumble readily in your fingers, which means they are usually between one to two years old – can be used as a mulch for your garden on bare ground to protect the soil during the winter or to maintain moisture around existing plants in the summer.

Dark brown crumbly mould with no sign of the original leaves indicates you have a collection of well-rotted leaf mould. An excellent seed-sowing mix, it provides a low-nutrient substrate with sufficient structure to help seeds sprout.

Potting compost can be made by combining equal parts well-rotted leaf mould, soil and garden compost to create a healthy, well-structured environment for your potted plants.

Me collecting leaf mould

CAN I MAKE LEAF MOULD WITHOUT ACCESS TO A FOREST OR PARK?

If you don't have access to leaf mould in your area, there are a few different and easy ways to make your own at home. The simplest method is to rake dry leaves up whenever you see them in your garden and pack them into a bin bag. Make sure to poke holes at the bottom and sides to allow the content to breathe. Store these leaves for one to two years until it turns into a dark brown substrate, which is usable leaf mould. However, I don't really like to use this method as it involves plastic bags.

My favoured method is:

1. Create a cage with chicken wire or netting and a single wooden structure as the base (a pallet works just fine).
2. Cover the pallet with wire mesh or similar to avoid materials falling through.
3. Make an upright hoop of the mesh that will sit on the pallet and secure the ends with cable ties.
4. Fill the cage up with leaves. Make sure they are moist. If they are really dry, water them and check every few months, repeating the process if you find any dry spots.

Remember that leaf mould takes a bit longer to decompose than most other organic substances as it's primarily decomposed by fungal activity. To speed up the process you could add something nitrogen-rich like grass clippings or coffee grounds and it will help to get leaf mould quicker.

Alternatively, shred the leaves into small bits and this will help to speed up the process. One of the main goals when having a garden is reducing your wastage, and dry leaves are no exception.

There are many more natural inputs that you could produce for your garden. To find out more, check out my videos online.

Rice and milk, used to make LAB (Lacto Acid Bacteria)

PART THREE

MAINTAINING YOUR GARDEN

WATERING YOUR GARDEN

WHY DO PLANTS NEED WATER?

Water is vital to plants just as it is to all life, including us. This is for many reasons. Water is needed to germinate seeds, to give the plant structure, help create energy through photosynthesis, soak up and deliver nutrients and moderate temperature.

Did you know that, like humans and horses, plants also sweat? The process is called transpiration. It occurs when plants take up water and nutrients from the soil and deliver these to the stem and leaves as part of the process of photosynthesis. The water then exits through pores called stomata and evaporates. As this happens, heat is removed from the air, which provides a cooling effect. This is why it can feel lovely and cool when you enter the woods on a really hot and muggy day.

If there isn't enough water the stomata close, which means they also stop taking in carbon dioxide and producing oxygen. The plant continues to heat up, it stops growing and, if it doesn't find water, it will eventually die. We don't want this to happen in your garden, so I have some great tips and tricks for you.

There is no need to go overboard with your garden and spend crazy amounts of money on complicated watering systems, especially in a small space where things are more manageable. It can be so easy to think you need all these expensive things to tend to your garden, but really you can get creative with what you already have or what family, friends and neighbours don't need anymore.

A FEW GOLDEN RULES FOR WATERING

Following a few golden rules for watering will really help you to establish your garden and help it to thrive in the long term.

1. There's no need to water your plants before planting, but water as soon as your plants are in the ground. This will encourage the roots to get in contact with the soil and become well established.

2. Don't water your plants in the heat of the day. The theory that plants can get burned if watered in full sunlight has been disproven, but it still isn't very efficient as more water evaporation will occur, which could lead to them not getting enough. I prefer to water either in the evening or in the morning as it gives the water lots of time to sink into the soil and for the plant to drink it. However, be careful of over-watering at night; it can cause the soil to become damp or waterlogged and lead to disease. If you water in the morning try to do it before the sun is too strong so it doesn't evaporate the water.

3. Try to water plants at the stem of the plant as opposed to the leaves, so that the water goes to where the plant needs it most. Watering only its leaves is a bit like washing your face when you are super thirsty.

4. When you water plants in pots, containers and hanging baskets, make sure you keep watering until the water lightly drips out the bottom of the pot – this is a sure sign that you have watered enough. Do not overdo this on your pots or you might risk flushing out much-needed nutrients.

Me watering the garden

Watering the plants

HOW DO I KNOW IF MY PLANTS NEED WATERING?

It's best to avoid over-watering plants, so learning about the different varieties and the behaviours they exhibit is vital. For example, some plants will wilt in full sun to preserve energy and then rehydrate later in the day, so may seem like they need watering, but are actually just conserving energy. Think of your plants as your friends – we all know that different friends act differently even in the same situations. Normally if the leaves are wilted and the soil is dry they are in need of water.

Also get to know the colour of your compost and soil. Is it paler than normal? Then the plant probably needs watering. If it is darker, you are at risk of over-watering them. Don't be afraid to stick your fingers into the soil. Using your finger to check a few centimetres below the surface to find out if the compost is dry is a really helpful guide to knowing if the plant needs more water.

If you still aren't quite sure after doing the above and your plants are in pots, you can check the weight of your pot. Simply lift your pot up as soon as you plant something in it. Repeat the lifting once you water your plant and notice the difference in weight. It takes a bit of practice but you can tell when your pot is light or heavy enough. This is particularly helpful when growing plants in pots that you move round the garden. Picking them up regularly really lets you get to know them by weight.

CREATING A WATERING SYSTEM

Keeping your small space watered can feel like one of the most challenging aspects of your garden. It can often feel like yet another thing on your to do list and that you are wasting a lot of water. Bought systems like sprinklers tend to do this, which isn't great for the environment or your water bill! But I have a few handy tricks and tips to really help you.

Creating a watering system using recycled materials is much more sustainable and more fun. This works really well if you are planning to go away for a few days. Here are my top DIY watering systems to help you.

DIY WATERING CAN

You will need:

- A plastic bottle with lid (any size)
- Nail and hammer

1. Poke holes in the cap.
2. Fill the bottle with water.
3. Use as a watering can.

This is particularly helpful when watering seedlings or newly planted seeds as it provides a light shower of water without disturbing the soil too much.

DIY watering system

SLOW-RELEASE WATERING SYSTEM (OLLA)

An Olla, pronounced "oh-yays", is a great, inexpensive way to keep your garden watered. They slowly release water using an ancient method. All you need is a terracotta pot, some blu tack (mounting putty) and a terracotta saucer to make your own.

They are fantastic watering systems for all types of plants. Terracotta pots are porous, allowing air and water to travel through them. Have you ever noticed a graveyard of terracotta pots with cracks? This is because they are porous and in winter they absorb water and the water inside freezes and causes the pots to break.

The top benefits of using an olla are that you are deep-watering your plant's roots where they really need it. It also reduces water use as you are only filling up the olla versus watering all the soil around it. It's fantastic for the soil, which gains moisture, as well as all the plants around the olla. The plant roots near the pot are aware of the moisture seeping through the terracotta and their roots grow towards the olla. Plants really are amazing. The best bit is that once you've installed it, you don't need to do anything except fill up your olla when it's dry.

They are really easy to make from simple terracotta pots and you don't need a timer or other tech to make them work. The only thing to remember is that it is important to seal the top of the olla to make sure water doesn't evaporate away

You will need:

- Terracotta pot with lid
- Blue tack (mounting putty)
- Terracotta saucer

DIY Olla
(full video on my
Instagram)

1. Add blue tack to seal the holes in the base of the pot so the water can't escape. It will just get slowly released by the porous pot instead.
2. Bury the pot in a convenient place among your plants so that the top of the pot is level with the surface of the soil.
3. Fill the buried pot with water so that it releases it slowly.
4. Don't forget to put your lid on to prevent evaporation and, hey presto: your very own DIY watering system!

SELF-WATERING POT

Self-watering pots are a great way to make sure you provide a consistent level of moisture to the roots of a plant. They are a great way to make sure your house plants, vegetables or herbs are watered if you are low on time or away. The best bit is they are super cheap to make – free, in fact, if you use recycled materials.

You will need:
- 2-litre (1⅓-gallon) plastic bottle
- Wick material (I used 100 per cent cotton from an old t-shirt)
- Soil and compost
- Water

1. Cut the plastic bottle in half horizontally.
2. Cut up your old cotton t-shirt into a long strip to make a long wick and feed this through the neck of the bottle.
3. Put the top half of your bottle upside down inside the base of the bottle.
4. Add compost mix in the top half.
5. Transplant your plant into the compost.
6. Fill up the bottom with water
7. Pop in a sunny space to grow.
8. Don't forget to check on it as you still need to fill it with water even though it waters itself!

DRIP IRRIGATION SYSTEM

A drip irrigation system is a great way to ensure your plants are well watered without having to spend lots of time doing it. Don't be too hands-off though – it is important to still spend time with your plants, as this is when you will see if they have a disease, a pest problem or are due a prune.

These systems can be really expensive to buy from a store, but you can make them yourself really cheaply using plastic bottles. I am showing you how to make a slow-release irrigation system but you could make this faster or even adjustable if you wanted.

You will need:
- A plastic bottle with cap (chose the right size bottle depending on the size of your space)
- Nails and a hammer or a drill
- Scissors or a stanley knife

1. Drill or hammer four to five holes in your bottle cap and a few smaller holes around the neck of the bottle. The more holes you add, the faster the irrigation system will be.
2. Cut the bottom off your plastic bottle.
3. Make a hole 10–15cm (4–6in) away from the plant's stem so the bottle can comfortably fit half way in. Be really careful to avoid your plant's roots.
4. Pop the bottle into the soil with the cap (secured on the bottle) face down. Pat into place.
5. Fill the bottle with water and leave it to drip irrigate your soil. Make sure there is nothing that could get stuck in the bottle opening to clog it up.
6. You can do this as many times as you like for the different plants in your garden.

MULCH

WHAT IS MULCHING?

For any extended period of time that I'm not at home, I get anxious about my garden. It can be tough for gardeners to vacation during the summer months because you'll be constantly worrying about the health of your plants, the shortage of water and other concerns.

Weeds can be controlled by covering the soil with mulch, which also acts as a barrier to drying winds and direct sunshine. Mulches are also a good source of slow-release nutrients. Mulch is consumed by worms and incorporated into the soil, which improves soil structure, moisture retention, free drainage and fertility.

There are a wide variety of mulches, both organic and inorganic, that can be used in the garden. Organic mulches include compost, leaves, bark and grass clippings. Non-organic mulches include plastic sheeting, landscaping fabric and "rubber mulch".

Unlike organic mulches, non-organic mulches do not disintegrate over time. With the passage of time, materials like plastic sheeting may deteriorate and endanger the environment in your garden. Additionally, soil nutrients may be prevented from reaching the soil in some cases by using non-organic mulches. Organic mulches, on the other hand, decompose quickly and may supply additional nutrients to your garden, making them a viable option.

Straw mulch to
apply in the garden

DIFFERENT TYPES OF MULCH

I use a variety of mulches in my garden, each of which has a different effect on my growing area. Even though it's not an easy undertaking, there are several strategies you can take to get the mulch you need without breaking the bank.

Compost

Soil mulch made from composted food waste, garden products and even manure is fantastic. Composting can be as simple as following the instructions outlined on page 125. Sourcing manure is another easy option, as there are many community farms in cities (I have three farms local in my area) and you just have to ask them if they can spare some manure. However, I rarely use manure in my garden.

Make sure your compost is thoroughly decomposed before applying it to your plants. It will provide the soil with a slow-release nutrition boost while insulating the roots from severe temperatures and enhancing drought tolerance.

It's also a good idea to use compost as a layer in between different types of mulch. Apply a small layer of mulch to the top of the soil, then cover it with another form of mulch, such as bark or wood chippings, for example. Compost not only provides protection for the micro- and macro-organisms but also improves the amount of organic matter in your garden, improves soil structure and adds biodiversity.

Wood Chippings

Mulch made of bark or wood chips is popular among gardeners because it is both inexpensive and visually appealing. Mulch made of these materials also aids in weed suppression, moisture retention and soil insulating.

Decomposing hardwood chippings are the best mulch for flower beds and borders because they decompose more quickly and enrich the soil biology. They look great in gardens and other natural environments as well. In general, pine wood chips, which have a higher acidity, take longer to decompose. Softwood chippings are better for trees and plants.

Wood chippings can be obtained for free if you live in a large city. What I usually do is to wait for tree surgeons to come and trim the trees in my street. They usually leave signs a few days before to warn people about parking restrictions for a certain date. Simply go and ask them if they could give you some and usually they will be happy to spare some for you. You are actually doing them a favour by collecting the wood chips so they don't have to dispose of them and they will have more room on the van. Make sure to bring a few bags with you.

I cover the entire floor of my urban garden with wood chippings even if it's made of concrete. It gives a much better look to the garden but it also has a few additional benefits. For example, when moving a small section of wood chippings from a concrete surface, there will usually be a lot of worms and other insects hiding under the first layer. This helps to improve the amount of biodiversity activity in your garden, aiding the ecosystem that you are trying to create. You can use this on your pathways, if you have open soil, to feed the micro and macro-organisms with organic matter.

Straw

Vegetable gardens and newly seeded lawns benefit greatly from the use of straw as a mulch. When applied in vegetable gardens, it provides a safe haven for spiders and other beneficial insects, which will help keep pests at bay.

Straw also prevents the lower leaves of vegetable plants from coming into contact with soil-borne diseases. For example, when you water your garden there's a sort of bounce-back effect from bare soil, which helps disease to spread all over your plants. By applying a thick layer of straw mulch, you reduce the bouncing effect and protect your plants.

Using straw mulch in the spring will save you a lot of time because it decomposes quite slowly, making it ideal as an organic mulch. As an example, strawberries or pumpkins can be grown without touching the ground thanks to the use of straw as a protective barrier. Because of the straw barrier, they will not become blemished if they are exposed to soil for a long period of time.

Straw also prevents newly sown seeds from being washed away or being eaten by rats and birds. Seeds germinate best when they have constant and continuous moisture, and straw is an excellent moisture-retentive material. It is also easy to clean up if you wish to move it away from the plants to create room for more, or it may be readily mixed into the soil.

When purchasing straw, keep in mind that if you buy hay by mistake, you could end up with a weed invasion in your garden as it is full of unhatched seeds that will come back to life as soon as you water your garden.

Sourcing straw in the city is not that easy. However, you could order it online or check on gumtree or ebay if anyone local to you is selling some. I usually buy straw online and use it mainly as mulch for my potatoes and garlic. I find a thick layer of straw on top of my potatoes or around the base of my garlic plants works perfectly to retain moisture and create ideal conditions for the plants to thrive and produce.

Seaweed

One of the best mulches for the garden can be found close to the sea or ocean, which is not only rich in nutrients, but also incredibly beneficial to the diversity of microorganisms in the soil. Sourcing seaweed in the city could be tricky but even a small amount is beneficial for your garden. I usually bring a few spare bags with me if I'm ever visiting the seaside and collect any seaweed that is not attached to a rock but has been washed up and is in the process of decomposition.

Seaweed is a great mulch, is nice to work with, deters slugs, adds minerals and nutrients to your soil and serves as a soil conditioner. Make sure to check the regulations in your area for how much seaweed could be collected. There's no need to wash it, and you can use it to mulch your garden, fresh or dry, or add it to your compost to decompose and increase the amount of nutrients and microorganisms. I've used seaweed as a mulch several times and haven't noticed any negative effects, such as a buildup of salt in the ground. Seaweed can be sprinkled on the driveway and hosed down before using as a mulch if you are concerned about salt. Allow a few weeks before planting something so the rain can wash the excess salt off your seaweed. If you are using freshwater lake weed, this will not be an issue.

Freshly harvested seaweed

Straw mulch to innoculate with mushroom spawn

HOW TO APPLY MULCH

It's pretty simple to spread mulch. The lower stems of your plants won't be harmed or smothered by the mulch you choose. You'll save time and work in the long run by preparing the soil first. Hand-pull or fork-pull annual and perennial weeds. Using a rake, straighten out any dips or holes in the soil, and then firm them up if necessary.

The soil should be well-watered before adding mulch so that the mulch can assist in retaining moisture. However, if you use something like straw, which could easily fly away on a windy day, I normally water it immediately after so that it sits in place.

Remember that weeds are deterred by light obstruction, but soil microbiology is also protected by a thick layer of mulch, creating a win-win situation.

Mulch can be applied using either a spade or your hands, depending on the type of mulch you have chosen. Make sure to also rake or hoe the mulch into a uniform layer that covers the soil.

INSECTS AND PESTS

BENEFICIAL INSECTS

With limited growing space in a small rebel garden there is less room for error, so knowing which insects are beneficial and which are garden pests is your key to success. However, don't reach for the pesticide, as you want your garden to be balanced by the wonder of nature.

Too many blackfly and greenfly, known as aphids, is a recurring issue every season for most gardeners, but what if we thought about it differently? Is it that we have too many aphids, but too few ladybirds? Do you have a mole problem, or simply not enough owls? Perhaps we need to install owl perches, where they can choose their dinner from?

Knowing which insects are good for your garden is vital. It means you can rely on nature keeping the balance and doing the hard work for you. It isn't just us small-scale gardeners that use them. Places like Thanet Earth in Kent, which has the biggest greenhouses in the whole of the UK (producing 400 million tomatoes a year) also use a system of predator control. This minimizes the use of pesticides, keeping both financial and environmental costs low. It is a great way to use nature to control pests in your garden, whatever the size. Predators help to manage pests, rather than pesticides that can kill the very insects that are trying to help, including the predators like ladybirds.

Here are seven insects you want to have in your garden.

HOVERFLIES (*DIPTERA: SYRPHIDAE*)

We often think of bees first when we think of pollinators but the hoverfly is a super-effective pollinator. A hoverfly is always welcomed and even encouraged in my garden. Some people confuse it with a bee because of its orange and brown markings and it even mimics the honeybee in the way it moves about using the same flight patterns. I promise this gardener's friend won't sting you! They do more than just pollinate as they also reduce biological materials and they control pests like aphids.

You can attract them by having plants that flower all year round, from ivy in the winter to fennel in the summer. One of the plants that seems most full of bees and hoverflies during summer is Sedum, and I keep a couple of varieties around the garden. Hoverflies, such as the common drone fly, are completely harmless to us and you can see them most of the year. They come out of hibernation on milder winter days.

CREATE A DIY HOVERFLY LAKE

You could even create a hoverfly lake. This is great to do with children, to show them the difference insects can make to the garden. Think of it like a water park for hoverflies!

Many species of hoverfly lay their eggs in water, which become rat-tailed, swimming maggots before turning into hoverflies. You can make your own hoverfly lake by repurposing materials you have at home.

1. Cut a large milk container in half with a stanley knife and fill it with rain water.
2. Add some leaves, grass and twigs. These will float and act as little platforms for female hoverflies to land on to lay their eggs.
3. It is best to put it in a shady spot so less water evaporates as it would in direct sunlight.
4. After a few weeks you should notice some rat-tailed maggots enjoying a swim. You have invited a natural predator for your aphids into your garden and also a brilliant pollinator.
5. Hoverflies also really like lemon balm, dill and marigolds, so you can also plant these to attract them.

LADYBIRDS (*COLEOPTERA*)

Ladybirds are a brilliant way to control aphids. In the past, I have bought ladybird larvae, which can eat up to 350–400 aphids in a three week period before turning into pupa and then a ladybird.

An adult ladybird can eat as many as 50 aphids a day, and it is estimated they consume an amazing 5,000 aphids over their lifetimes. So you can really see why the ladybird is a gardener's friend!

To control your aphids and blackfly you can buy ladybird larvae, which will come in a small box with a release bag. Simply empty the whole contents of the box inside the release bag. Within 7–10 days they will emerge from the release bag and start eating the pests around your garden. Make sure to source native ladybirds if you are planning to buy some for your garden.

LADYBIRD FACTS

- You may not even realize you have ladybird larvae in your garden. Some people say they look like mini alligators.
- Did you also know ladybirds are cannibals and will eat each other if there aren't enough aphids in the garden to eat?
- Ladybirds will also lay infertile eggs as a source of protein for their ladybird larvae to snack on.
- Do you know where the name for Ladybirds came from? It has been said that in the Middle Ages crops in Europe were plagued by pests. So, like any good farmer in the Middle Ages, they took to praying to the Virgin Mary for a solution. What happened next was that ladybirds started to arrive and eat the pests, saving their crops. This led to the farmers calling the red and black beetles "our lady's birds" or "lady beetles". In Germany the name for them is *marienkafer*, which translates to "Mary Beetles".

Ladybird

PARASITIC WASPS (*HYMENOPTERA*)

These stingless wasps are your partners in fighting pests in your garden. It may feel odd to want to attract wasps to your garden, but they play a really important role and eat so many garden beasts, from those brassica-munching caterpillars to aphids.

Female parasitic wasps look like they have a stinger but it is actually an ovipositor, which they use to pierce insects and leave her eggs inside. Then when the eggs hatch they feed inside the host for a little while before cutting a hole to escape through. Nature's wonderful, isn't it?

It can be hard to spot these wasps in the garden but you can notice what they leave behind. If you have a known area of aphids in your garden, look to see if there are any that have turned crusty and golden brown or black. These are mummified aphids and are a brilliant sign that parasitic wasps are doing the job you want and need them to in your garden.

They really love coriander (cilantro), marigolds and fennel, as well as bolting brassicas or dill flowers. So these are great to interplant or put around a border to attract parasitic wasps and manage any pests in your garden. You can even buy them to be released into your garden but make sure you have plants they can feed from and pollinate first. They are often used on an industrial scale in farming and are released in greenhouses and fields.

VIOLET GROUND BEETLES (*COLEOPTERA: CARABIDAE*)

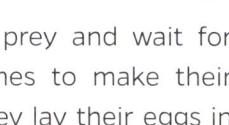

These magnificent creatures are busy working hard, devouring pests in your garden while you sleep. If you are lucky enough to spot one of them lazing under a log or stone in the day or snug under some leaves you will notice their stunning metallic purple sheen.

They are quite gross in the way they consume pests, such as snails and slugs. They vomit on their prey and wait for their digestive enzymes to make their food easier to eat! They lay their eggs in the soil, which is another reason I use the no-dig method (see page 20) so I don't disturb predators like this who really are an organic grower's best friend.

LACEWING (*CHRYSOPERLA*)

These are brilliant for smaller gardens as they will be as at home in a hanging basket or a herb garden as they are in larger areas like woodland or meadows. They are pretty beautiful, too, when you see them close up. They have bright green bodies with metallic eyes with their beautiful transparent wings decorated with green veins that look like lace.

They may look beautiful but, like the ladybirds, they are pretty ferocious predators of aphids and aphid larvae. So much so they have been nicknamed "aphid lion". It is like having your own army in the garden to take on the aphids. It is the babies, the lacewing larvae, that do the heavy lifting – they can feast on around 200 aphids a week! You can make your own lacewing lair for the garden (see box below), or you can buy the larvae or eggs online or at a garden centre near you.

Did you know that adult lacewing ears are at the base of their wings? The reason for this is so they can hear bat echolocation signals. This is their cue to shut their wings so they appear smaller and avoid being dinner.

LACEWING DIY LAIR

If you want to encourage lacewings into your garden you can make them their very own lair to overwinter in using recycled materials. A plastic bottle is perfect.

1. Cut the bottom off a plastic boottle, keeping it as smooth as possible so you don't cut yourself.
2. Roll up some corrugated cardboard and push it into the bottle.
3. Cut two holes opposite each other at the base of the bottle to stick a twig through The twig is there to stop the cardboard falling out, so make sure it fits in snugly.
4. Unscrew the lid and add some string using the lid to secure it in place.
5. Find somewhere to hang it in your garden. Lacewings like to be warm in their lair so hang it somewhere with shelter, such as a tree or near your house, ideally about 1.8m (6ft) off the ground.

BEES (*ANTHOPHILA*)

Where would we be without bees! There are so many different types, from the well-known bumblebee to the honeybee with its wonderful waggle dance. Popular vegetables, such as broccoli, asparagus and cucumber, and fruits like strawberries, tomatoes and blackberries, rely upon bees to pollinate them.

They are so important that it has been estimated that it would cost farmers in the UK an incredible £1.8 billion per year to manually pollinate their crops. Yet using pesticides, such as neonicotinoids, are really impacting them. The poor bee comes along to pollinate the plant and then ingests the pesticide along with the nectar, which can seriously damage the bee's central nervous system.

Planting flowers attracts bees to your garden, as does having flowering veg and allowing some things, like chives, to go to bolt. Also, plants like lavender attract the wonderful bee that will help you produce higher yields, especially in small spaces.

Bee on a dahlia

BUILD A DIY BEE HOTEL

You can buy ready-made bee hotels or you could build your own using recycled materials. These are perfect for solitary bees, who don't live in a hive, as the name suggests.

They like to build their nests alone, usually in tunnels, hollow stems and beetle holes. So why not make it easy for them to check into your garden and build a hotel for them to stop off at and lay their eggs.

1. Chop a plank of untreated wood that is at least 10cm (4in) wide into five pieces. Three of these should be of equal size to create a rectangle frame that will support the roof. Two pieces need to be cut at a right angle so you can create a nice sloping roof. You will want one to be slightly longer than the other so you can slot them together at a 90-degree angle.
2. Drill some guide holes for the screws to go in, to hold your frame together.
3. Cut some reeds, bamboo canes and hollow stems to match the depth of the frame. You can use a saw, but if you don't have one a pair of garden secateurs should do the trick.
4. Pack them into the frame.
5. If you have underestimated how many you need, don't panic. You could cut up some fallen wood into circles and a few holes to add to the frame. You could also add another piece of wood and name your DIY Bee Hotel to add something a bit different to your space.
6. Now all you have to do is hang it up in a sunny spot where it is also sheltered from any rain. Have a coffee and wait for your first guests to check in. Remember they won't be booking a double room, as they are solitary!

DIY insect hotel

SPIDERS (*ARANEAE*)

If you are an arachnophobe you may struggle with this one, but spiders are an essential companion in the fight against pests in your garden. One of the best things about them is that they show up early as they overwinter in your garden hidden under gardening debris. They are first to show up to the party, ready to devour pests that arrived without an invite. They spin their hammock, aka web, and get straight to snacking on unwanted garden guests.

The only downside is they aren't able to decipher the wanted from the unwanted guests. They are not picky eaters and you may find a bee trapped in their web.

How to invite spiders in
Spiders, such as the wolf spider, like to make their homes in mulch so they can hide before mounting their attack. Having a no-dig garden really helps with this as you aren't disturbing them. Also, don't over tidy your garden in winter so they have places to overwinter ready to greet your unwanted pests in spring.

Spider in a web

GARDEN PESTS

There are many garden pests that enter your garden and, while beneficial insects can really help keep them at bay, there are other environmental solutions too, from planting flowers to attract pests away from your produce and leaving your garden crop undisturbed, to simply having to stand there and pick some of the pests by hand. The most important thing is that your garden doesn't become infested before the balance of nature is restored.

FUNGUS GNATS (*SCIARID FLIES*)

Fungus gnats are one of the worst enemies for your houseplants and seedlings. Adults live for 7–10 days and a female can lay up to 100–300 eggs in batches of 2–30! Fungus gnats are a pest of plants in pots and trays. The adults crawl over the compost surface and, if disturbed, fly on the lower leaves. The larval stage in the compost attacks the roots and can kill young seedlings, which isn't something anyone wants.

You can protect your plants by using beneficial nematodes, which are natural parasites of insects. Sciarid nematodes are roundworms that are classified as macro-biological organisms, which prefer to live on the soil and only like to feed on specific insects. They move through the soil to locate a host insect and enter through natural openings. I will leave the rest to your imagination!

Fungus gnats caught on a sticky trap

DIY FUNGUS GNAT DETERRENT

You will need:

- A pack of sciarid nematodes
- 11 litres (3 gallons) rain water or unchlorinated water
- A measuring jug
- Large bucket
- A watering can
- Yellow sticky traps or potatoes

1. Mix the whole packet of sciarid nematodes into 1 litre (4 cups) of the water.
   I used a kitchen measuring jug to do this. You can't over-apply, so don't worry!
2. Add this to the remaining water in a watering can and apply
   liberally to your plants so there is run-off water.
3. Then put up yellow sticky traps, which you can get from a local nursery,
   garden centre or buy online. I attached mine to cable ties and hung them
   up in the greenhouse, but you could use wooden skewers or sticks, too.
4. Another natural thing that fungus gnat larvae love is raw potato chunks. So you
   could cut up some potato chunks and add them to your pots. It is a great way
   to check for larvae and trap them away from the plant roots at the same time.
5. Make sure you check your pots or beds and remove infested
   chunks. Chuck them away and replace with fresh ones.

SLUGS AND SNAILS

The Royal Horticultural Society declared these are the top pests in the garden. The sale and use of slug pellets is now officially banned in the UK since the new legislation came into force on 1 April 2022. You could now technically eat a garden snail in the UK as long as you prepared it properly. If you don't want to eat them, though, there are still a few natural ways to control this pest. You could line your borders with eggs shells or sand, as this prevents them from gliding past.

You can use plants, such as strong-smelling mint, geraniums, chives, garlic or fennel, to deter them. They don't like these plants at all. Seaweed mulch is also a great way to deter them. As is going out there and picking them out by hand. It is surprising how many you can find. I sometimes go out at night with a head torch to spot as many as I can, trap them in a bucket and relocate as far as possible, usually at the local park.

Top: Slugs and snails picked from the garden
Bottom: Vine weevil

VINE WEEVILS

Vine weevils are particularly partial to munching on plants grown in containers, so they often appear indoors or in small spaces. They can quickly infest lots of plants so get out there quickly and pick them off in the evening by torchlight or even moonlight.

For smaller plants, you can try shaking them over an upside down umbrella or newspaper. You can also trap adults by putting a sticky barrier around your pots as well as encouraging birds, frogs and hedgehogs into your garden, though this is slightly trickier if you are growing them inside or on a balcony. I am not sure my cats would know what to do if they saw a hedgehog coming to visit my home.

REPELLING CATS AND FOXES

I am going to tell you how to do this without using any sort of chemical at all – just as nature intended. I know it can be frustrating when you have unwanted visitors in your garden digging up your plants. Even invited ones, like your own cats, getting up to mischief can be irritating as they undo the good work you have done. To understand how to naturally repel them we firstly need to understand them.

FOX AND CAT BEHAVIOURS

Foxes can be found everywhere, in both urban and rural areas. Adapting to our ever-changing landscape is no problem for foxes, as they are extremely intelligent. They can be found in the countryside as well as in cities like London, where I currently reside.

The foxes that roam the countryside and cities are always on the lookout for new and exciting things to eat. When it comes to territory, wild foxes and domestic cats are vastly different. Foxes spend the majority of their day scent-marking and patrolling in order to keep their territory free of other invading foxes.

For a cat, the battle for territory is not a matter of life and death, unlike for a fox, in the greater scheme of things. Of course, a cat's behaviour toward a neighbour's cat could be upsetting to the owner who believes their cat is being bullied. If things get uncomfortable, a domestic cat knows that its owner will provide food and that he or she can always retreat to the safety of the house. Wild foxes, on the other hand, are completely self-sufficient. It doesn't have the convenience of a tasty meal or a cosy couch to curl up on. This means that foxes are extremely cautious. They will leave the area immediately if they detect even the slightest hint of danger. It's a matter of life and death for them.

I have been dealing with urban foxes for about seven years and I have learned a few tips to avoid issues in the garden. I have found an ideal way to keep foxes away: by giving plants a strong smell! I have tried lots of homemade remedies and my homemade repellent spray is by far the most effective, and an added bonus is that it is really easy to make! Of course, I combine a few other things like sensor lights and sometimes lions' poo which you can buy from any garden centre.

HOMEMADE REPELLENT SPRAY

This strongly smelling mix of herbs could help to repel foxes and other kinds of animals. However, try to implement different techniques to keep them away from your garden. Repeat the process every two weeks, or after heavy rain, as the smell wears off.

You will need :
- 1.5 litres (6 cups) water
- 1 cup basil leaves, chopped
- 1 cup geranium leaves, chopped
- 4 garlic cloves (or a large onion), chopped
- 1 cup sage leaves, chopped

1. Heat the water in a large pan on your stove. Bring it to a simmer so it is almost boiling but not quite.
2. Add the basil, geranium, garlic and sage to the pan.
3. Turn the heat down to low and add a lid. Leave the mixture to simmer for about 30 minutes. Remove the pan from the heat and leave to cool.
4. Strain the cold mixture through a strainer and separate the solids from the liquid.
5. Use a funnel to pour the liquid into a spray bottle or sprayer. You can use the strained solids around your garden
6. Spray your garden including your fence and other areas.

ORGANIC PEST CONTROL METHODS

When the weather warms up, pollinators are finally starting to wake up and return to the garden. Even in the healthiest gardens, bugs will inevitably arrive, but not all insect damage is substantial enough to warrant treatment.

The best method to keep your garden healthy is to educate yourself and learn how to recognize typical "bad pests". It is easier to manage a pest using environmentally friendly approaches if it is recognized as soon as possible.

Every gardener must deal with insect problems from time to time, and it is critical to learn how to deal with pests invading your garden without using chemical pesticides.

When I first started gardening, I was anxious about bugs in the garden and would react by applying harsh chemicals that would kill any insect in the garden without distinguishing between useful pollinators and pests, disrupting the natural biodiversity of my growing space.

"Farmers are thought to be the primary users of pesticides to treat their crops. In actual fact, homeowners use around three times as many pesticides as farmers."

Some chemicals have an impact on the entire food chain, not just pests and pollinators. For example, if a mouse consumes an insect that has been treated with a persistent pesticide, and the owl eats the mouse, the owl will absorb some of the poison.

There are several organic methods for controlling pests in your garden that are easy yet efficient in maintaining a natural balance.

What I have learned from Jadam and Mr. Cho's studies on Korean Natural Farming (see page 22) is to observe and learn from nature. What I mean is that you should simply watch and look, and smell! In particular, notice which plants have a strong natural odour. These plants often have repellent properties for many pests in your garden. Some actually attract pests and mask the scent or the presence of the rest of your vegetable plants, saving them from the munching menace! You don't need chemicals; the plants around you could be used to develop a powerful pest repellent solution.

"TRAP CROPS"

There are many different plants that could be planted in your garden to improve production and flavour or repel nasty bugs. Over the years I've been experimenting with different plant combinations. Through research, trial and error, and studying their symbiotic effects, I have managed to fight pests naturally without applying any man-made chemicals in my growing space. I'm here to say it is possible!

Nasturtiums

This plant is completely edible, including flowers, stems, leaves and seeds. It has a strong peppery flavour, which you could either love or hate. Nasturtium is also called a sacrificial plant or "trap crop" due to its ability to attract green and black flies (also called aphids), which literally raid the plant. However, you need to be careful when using these plants as the aphids could easily jump to your vegetables close by, so don't grow them directly next to the plant you are trying to save from aphids.

The main issue is with ants, since ants feed on aphid honeydew and literally farm them. Ants usually move aphids to different plants so they can reproduce and provide more food. What you want to do is to make their life hard so they will move elsewhere. However, it is not always possible to do this, so I recommend using nematodes directly, which could sort the problem after a few applications without harming your garden and the natural biodiversity.

Marigolds

This is another perfect example of a "trap crop". I plant it mainly among tomatoes or the nightshade family, which includes aubergines (eggplant), potatoes and peppers.

There are over fifty marigold (*Tagetes*) species. The three most popular for use in the garden are African marigold (*T. erectus*), French marigold (*T. patula*) and Signet marigold (*T. tenuifolia*). They have many advantages like attracting beneficial pollinators. They provide a natural pest control by producing a strong smell that masks the scent of your vegetables from pests and deters moths from laying their eggs on your vegetable plants. They also act as a "trap crop" for slugs and snails.

I usually plant them either in between my tomato plants or around the whole border to create a barrier, which should mask the scent of my vegetables. This is best done three to four weeks before planting tomatoes, as their roots will create a symbiotic relationship with the roots of the tomato plant, repelling root knot nematodes, which could wipe out your entire crop.

Amaranth

This is an excellent "trap crop" for your garden, which also makes an incredible display and is really versatile in the kitchen. The leaves are edible and also the seeds, which could be turned into flour or for a delicious breakfast porridge.

Amaranth attracts cucumber beetles, and so it's recommended to plant a wall of beautiful amaranth around the edge of your garden to keep your cucumbers, squash and other cucurbits (gourd family) free from this pest. However, be careful where you plant your amaranth because when it flowers and goes to seed, it will drop lots of seeds all over the ground and almost certainly you will have amaranth the year after.

Left: Red amaranth
Right: Nasturtiums growing in the garden

USING PLANTS TO CONTROL PESTS

Many pests (such as carrot root fly, white fly and aphids) can be deterred simply by planting a row of strong-smelling plants adjacent to a row of sensitive vegetables.

Herbs and flowers are excellent companion plants for your growing space, and they help to prevent and repel garden pests, which otherwise may mean the end of your efforts to grow your own food.

The easiest method to get all of the plants you need to keep pests away from your garden is to start from seeds. The reason I recommend starting from seed is that it is firstly much more convenient but also many garden centres use chemicals to grow their plants, which you don't want to transfer into your garden, as well as pests that could be on the plants and introduced into your growing space. It may appear to be costly, which is why many garden growers choose the simple option of using chemical pesticides. Pesticides, on the other hand, are never cheap, and the damage they cause might last for years or even be permanent. Ultimately, we want to cooperate with nature to create an environment that encourages insect and microbial biodiversity to flourish.

Before the season begins, I usually make a list of the plants I wish to grow and the pests that can harm them. Each plant has a wealth of knowledge readily available via a simple internet search. This list helps me identify pest-repellent plants, as well as their heights, so that I may place them where they will get the most sun. Finally, I do a rough design of where I plan to put each of the plants I'll be using.

Even if it seems like a lot of work, you only have to do this once. Your planting diary will serve as an annual reference guide from then on. In order to demonstrate how to build a comparable list, here is a template that I adapted to my needs:

Plant:
Tomato

Pests:
Aphids, budworm, cutworms, looper caterpillars, two-spotted mite or red spider mite, root-knot nematode, thrips, tomato russet mite or tomato mite.

Repelling plants:
Marigold, geraniums, mint or thyme, dill, basil, cosmos

Notes:
Birds will take care of the insects that the companion plants can't repel

Choose the plants that will keep pests away from your garden and make sure to match the ideal plant for your growing area based on the amount of space you have available. Just remember that the more plants you have in your growing area, the better your chances are of keeping pests at bay and maintaining a pest-free garden.

You don't have to stick to the same exact list but you can experiment with different species and grow according to your needs. In pest management, failure is part of the learning process, and you can always try again the following year and learn something new. I've lost many plants over the course of my gardening journey, but it is all part of the learning experience and I managed to unearth a lot of useful information.

The Top Plants section at the end of this book includes pest-repellent plants that I rigorously plant in my garden every season to control and reduce the amount of pests and their damage on my crop.

 ## PEST REPELLENT SOLUTION

Creating your own natural pesticides at home is an easy technique that may be used to prevent an infestation or treat one that has already started. Homemade pesticides are not only easier to make, but they are also less expensive and better for the environment than many commercial alternatives. Insecticide can be made from household things that you already own. Pests in the garden can be deterred or eliminated with a surprising number of natural and safe solutions.

Testing on a small piece of the plant before using a home mix can guarantee that the plant is not harmed. On a hot or sunny day, avoid spraying any plants with a homemade mixture because this can quickly cause the plants to burn and perish. Always spray your plants either early in the morning or late in the day to give the plant enough time to absorb the liquid before the hot hours of the day.

DIY FERMENTED STINGING NETTLE AND GARLIC TEA

The presence of stinging nettles (*Urtica dioica*) as companion plants may help fruit trees, roses and tomatoes, since their active compounds are known to prevent pests like thrips. However, growing this plant among your primary crops is probably not a good idea because it might sting you rather frequently.

The popularity of fermented stinging nettle tea has increased in recent years due to its organic and natural properties; it is really potent. In my garden I always face issues with green and black flies (aphids) but I had a noticeable difference by applying nettles and garlic combined. Visit your local park, woods or one of the many walkways and regions in the city or suburbs for easy access to wild nettles. To get the highest concentration of acids from nettles, harvest them early in the season by trimming off the tender green top stems. In the course of fermentation, a variety of acids and lectin proteins are released from the plant. To keep aphids at bay, you need to combine acids and lectins, which disturb their growth cycle.

Me holding some nettles

I normally begin producing this at the beginning of the season in early spring, when the nettles begin to emerge from their overwintered seeds in the ground. When working with nettles, always use rubber gloves. While it's possible to avoid getting stung without gloves, it's better to avoid it.

Local stores often give away old, recycled plastic buckets that they no longer need. If you're going to use old buckets, be sure to thoroughly rinse and wash them to get rid of any leftover materials. Metal buckets should not be used as they react with the mixture.

I normally use rainwater or unchlorinated/filtered water to dilute 1kg (2lb) nettles. The bacteria that grows during the fermentation process may be killed by chlorine. It is possible to obtain unchlorinated water by simply using tap water that has been left out in the open air for at least 48–72 hours.

If you grow your own garlic like me, you can keep all the small cloves or bad-looking bulbs and use them for this process. Alternatively, if you have a trusted source of organic garlic, such as an organic food store close by, you can buy some to use in this recipe. I'd suggest peeling around 3–5 full bulbs of garlic and crushing them to add to your recipe. It is really important to crush the garlic and wait for about 10 minutes before using the cloves. During this time the maximum amount of allicin will be released. Fresh garlic contains the chemical alliin. Chopping or crushing the clove releases an enzyme called alliinase. Alliin is converted to allicin by this enzyme. This is a defensive mechanism of garlic, which helps to repel most small flying or crawling insects like aphids, mites, beetles, slugs, mosquitoes and flies.

A cheesecloth or muslin with a rock or weight inside will keep the leaves, stems and garlic from floating to the surface. Make sure to strip off all the leaves before adding them to the bag. Submerge the bag and cover the bucket to prevent it from leaking out. Allow the mixture to steep for at least a week or two, checking on it every other day. Keep it out of the way of your doors if you don't want it to stink up the place!

Once the solution is ready, I dilute it 50:50 with filtered or unchlorinated water. You can spray it directly on your plants, making sure to coat the top and bottom of every leaf. This will ensure a rapid absorption of the liquid. Check the weather predictions so you don't risk spraying your plant before the rain. Ideally you would give the plants a couple of days to absorb the scent of nettles and garlic. You can compost the remaining pulp of nettles.

You can also use this mixture as a liquid fertilizer by simply diluting it with water (40 to 50 per cent tea-to-water ratio) and pouring it on the ground as a soil drench.

 ## BENEFICIAL NEMATODES

Another method that could help you get rid of pests in the garden are Nematodes. Nematodes are microscopic creatures that act as parasites on other insects. They release bacteria into the host's body to kill them. The nematode then eats the host. For the organic grower, this is a biological, not chemical, pest control. Unlike a chemical spray, which may drift off target, nematodes are specific to the host pest, so that other wildlife is not affected.

You can buy nematodes online. However, they aren't necessarily cheap and you do need to follow the very precise instructions on how to use them. To use nematodes, it is important to choose the correct nematode for the right type of pest. And to use them in the right conditions.

- The soil needs to be above 5°C (41°F) – and will remain so, even at night.
- The pests or their larvae need to be active.
- Nematodes should be applied when light levels are low. They are light-sensitive, so apply them in the very early morning or at dusk.

A few years ago I had a fungus gnat (see page 181) infestation in my house due to the high level of humidity around some plants that started from seed indoors, under grow lights. I tried to get rid of them using many methods but the only possible option in the end was nematodes. I did a couple of applications on the affected plants and all the other plants in the house just in case. I saw a noticeable reduction of gnats and I almost stopped having any throughout the whole growing season. However, I personally tried nematodes just a single time so I can't guarantee the long-term effectiveness of them.

JADAM HERBAL SOLUTION (JHS)

You might think of Jerusalem artichokes as just an edible vegetable, but they actually have a fascinating use in Jadam Natural Farming (see page 22). The best use for Jerusalem artichokes is by making a natural pesticide called Jadam Herbal Solution (JHS).

Other vegetables or flowers can be used to make JHS, but I like to use Jerusalem artichokes as they are a perennial plant that is easily grown and available anywhere in the world. Tuber length and width range from 7–10cm (3–4in). They have light brown skin with red, yellow or purple undertones covering white flesh. Although they make good food for us, they do have some poisonous properties.

You will need:
- 700g (1½lb) Jerusalem artichokes, cut into pieces
- 5 litres (1 gallon) water
- Mesh bag

1. Place the artichokes in a mesh bag in a large pan with the water. Weigh the bag down so that the artichokes stay submerged.
2. Bring the water to the boil, then lower it to medium and maintain a boiling temperature. I recommend doing this outside if you are using herbs or plants with a strong smell. I did mine outdoors, as I wanted to try out my fire pit, which I built recycling a few bricks that one of my neighbours was about to chuck away, and it was also a great excuse to later have a barbecue!
3. Boil for around five hours, topping up the water once it evaporates to half the size of your pot.
4. Strain the whole mixture while still boiling hot and put into a heat-resistant bottle. Be careful when doing this and use all the necessary protections like heat-resistant gloves.
5. Seal the bottle immediately and store it on its side for later use. By laying it on its side, you will keep the hot liquid in contact with the cap to seal and sterilize it. If you stand it up, there will be a bubble of air between them.

When using the JHS you do not want to use the sediments, so make sure to filter it before using if it is not clear. Use this mixture diluted 1:100 to 1:20 starting low (mix with unchlorinated or filtered water).

Caution:

It is important that a home mixture never be applied to any plant on a hot or bright sunny day, as this will quickly lead to burning of the plant and its ultimate demise.

You can make many different kinds of JHS to use as pesticide, but it's recommended not to mix different plants. Keep your inputs separate and mix them up in the same solution before spraying your plants.

I usually make a few different ones to use in the season: juniper, lavender and garlic. The best way to understand if a plant could be used for this process is to observe how it interacts with insects in nature. As a rule of thumb, strong-scented plants are usually great to use. Any sort of plant that insects avoid has potential to be pesticidal. If the mixture goes bad and starts smelling bad, you can always dilute it 1:1,000 and use it as a soil drench to enhance the growth of plants instead. Remember that we are using natural inputs so it's really unlikely to cause irreversible damage to your garden and it's worth experimenting with what you manage to create.

In order to make your JHS effective, you need a wetting agent. Any pesticide needs to coat, wet and penetrate into the target pest to be effective. This is also called JWA (Jadam Wetting Agent). However, I don't make my own but I buy this online (you can source it from many natural farming websites) as during the production process a lot of heat is released due to the use of potassium hydroxide. JWA combined with JHS can help to control issues such as aphids, mealybugs, mites, leafhoppers, scale insects, caterpillars, thrips, whitefly, powdery mildew and more.

There are also other kinds of natural inputs that could be combined with Jadam Herbal Solution to deter pests even more effectively but I'm still experimenting myself.

Jadam Herbal Solution in the making

ESSENTIAL TOOLS

WHAT TOOLS WILL YOU NEED?

There is a lot of information out there if you want to start gardening, but it might be a little intimidating when it comes to choosing the right tools to take care of your growing space. Essential gardening tools for beginners are not really that hard to find – and they don't have to fill up an entire shed either.

When you're a novice gardener, the options for tools, equipment and supplies might seem endless. The most experienced gardener, on the other hand, is likely to have a basic collection of tools that they rely on throughout the year. Most beginner gardeners usually get to the garden centre and end up spending a lot of money on unnecessary stuff. I like to have a few tools in my collection.

It's important to keep them sharp and clean at all times if you want them to last for a long time. Simply clean the handle and bottom part of each tool with a cloth whenever you finish using them in your garden. I also use a sharpening stone once in a while to keep my shovel, spade, trowel, knife, secateurs, hedge shears and a few others sharpened up and ready to use.

Luckily for you, I've put together a list of tools that I wish I knew I needed when I started growing my own food.

Copper trowel and
Copper dibber

SPADE/SHOVEL

A spade is the perfect compromise between a trowel and a shovel. It is mainly used to dig holes around the garden to make space for a plant. However, it also helps in shovelling soil, compost and organic fertilizer out of a pit, container or wheelbarrow, cutting a trench or slicing off thick turf.

If you are planning to have a raised bed garden like mine, it is one of the main tools you'll need. I also own a shovel that I use when I need to move a pile of wood chippings, soil or compost. It can be used to chop off small tree roots, so make sure to keep it sharp all the time.

The simple difference between a spade and a shovel is that a shovel is primarily used for scooping and moving materials from one place to another and is generally larger than spades so that more material can be moved with each scoop.

GARDENING GLOVES

These come in different materials. A lot of people think they won't need gloves for the garden, but aubergines (eggplant), courgettes (zucchini) and many other common plants could be a pain if they were handled without a good pair of gloves. I use them for many tasks and I recommend investing a few extra pounds when getting a pair of gloves as they will protect your precious hands.

TROWEL

A trowel is perfect for weeding and planting small plants, preparing a small flower bed and getting compost or organic fertilizer out of a container. It is one of the most versatile tools in your garden and it's always good to have one or two laying around and ready to be used. There are many different kinds of trowel out there, but I have had a scoop trowel for about three years now and it's good for pretty much anything. With proper maintenance, it could last you a while. Just make sure to wash it and clean it with a cloth after every use.

SECATEURS

The pruning and tidying of plants is a regular garden task, and a pair of secateurs will become one of your most useful pieces of kit. Secateurs are used mainly for light pruning, cutting flower stems and tidying broken plants. Garden clippers – a bit like scissors – which can be operated with one hand are a worthwhile investment and will set you up for seasons to come. There are two kinds of secateurs – bypass secateurs and anvil secateurs. The former is for general pruning, while the anvil works best for cutting branches or hard stuff.

 ## MICRO TIP PRUNERS

These are ideal for shaping, trimming and for intricate snipping in tight places. The blades are usually made from quality stainless steel that cut all the way to the tip, and a soft grip handle that works for both left and right-handed users. Pruning is perfect for encouraging healthy growth on plants and flowers. I also use them to remove suckers from the tomato plants, top off my chilli plants or prune the bottom part of some plants.

 ## RAKE

A rake's main purpose is for the upkeep of the garden by collecting leaves, trash, debris and other piles to prevent clutter. It helps in levelling a flower bed or dragging large stones off a planting bed. I also use a rake whenever I'm mulching to have an even layer of mulch covering my raised beds. There are mainly two kinds of rakes – a leaf rake or a bow rake. A bow rake is generally considered the best for levelling dirt, sand and other materials that are heavier than leaves. A leaf rake is used mainly to gather leaves from gardens and paths.

 ## DIBBER

A dibber is a pointed wooden or metal stick that is used to dig a hole with minimal disturbance for the soil microorganisms and fungal network. I've got my dibber from Charles Dowding, which is designed differently to the standard ones. It is more round and not so pointed so you can use it to draw shallow lines on your raised beds to guide your planting in straight lines.

FORK

An efficient tool for turning soil, garden forks can dig into dense soil better than a spade. A digging fork has four to six tines that are flat, with no curvatures. Its function is just as its name suggests, for digging, and it is especially good for compacted clay or rocky beds. The strong tines of the digging fork are able to penetrate problem soils that a spade can have trouble cutting into. As well as digging up the ground, a good fork can simply loosen up the area before digging with a spade. Either way, using a digging fork will reduce the strain on your body. Sometimes I use it to turn my compost pile.

 ## HEDGE SHEARS

The next tool that I'd highly recommend is garden hedge shears. I use them mainly to cut unwanted ivy growing along my fence, but you could also use it to prune trees or tall plants. Hedge shears look a lot like giant scissors with their long pair of straight blades. They are designed to help you cut as much of a plant as possible in one single sweep. When you use hedge shears, they will create long, sharp edges on whatever you trim. This makes them perfect for maintaining shaped hedges. However, hedge shears are not great at shaping bushes and plants with strong wooden branches. I also use them to chop plant materials before adding them to my compost pile so it decomposes faster.

 ## WATERING CAN

Watering cans are another essential item for the garden. I have a few with 8–10 litre (2–2.6 gallon) capacities. To keep seedlings and young plants refreshed, a watering can with a "rose" (the sprinkler attachment on the end of the watering spout) will distribute water lightly and evenly. It's pretty common in big cities to not have water directly connected to your garden so this could be one of the main tools for your small garden space. I usually refill a water tank every week or so and use my watering can to hand water my whole garden.

WHEELBARROW (OPTIONAL)

If your backyard has extra soil to be moved around, compost or mulch that needs to be added to garden beds, or any other heavy lifting and moving projects, a wheelbarrow can help you haul hundreds of pounds. I bought mine not long ago from the local tool store, and I wish I had bought it years ago. I used it many times to carry home wood chippings kindly offered by the gardeners at the local park and it's absolutely great if you are based in a city with limited access to resources.

 ## SHARPENING STONE

I also got a sharpening stone for maintenance of edge tools with two different grades of coarseness for shaping and fine tuning, to ensure the sharpest and cleanest of edges. It is really easy to use and it costs only a few pounds. I highly recommend keeping your tools clean after each use and ideally storing them in a covered location from rain and humidity.

THE ADVANTAGES OF COPPER TOOLS

Copper tools are pretty expensive compared to average garden tools, but they are worth it in the long run and they come with a variety of benefits which help to control pests and nurture plants.

Slugs and snails have blood based on copper, which means they don't have an independent magnetic field and so are more sensitive to the earth's magnetic force. Using non-copper tools to turn the soil leaves a "signature" in the magnetic field. Snails and slugs can detect these signatures; they come at night, following the lines of magnetic field, and they will stop where you disturbed it, eating your plants.

In addition to this, copper tools have a much longer life span compared to other tools. They are extremely light and sharp, so it is easier to slice into the ground. By using copper tools, you will find that they start to release micro pieces of copper into your soil. This a good thing for your plants. Copper is a key component of many enzyme systems and stimulates several plant enzymes involved in the formation of lignin. It is also necessary for the process of photosynthesis, plays a crucial role in plant respiration, and facilitates the metabolism of proteins and carbohydrates in plants.

TYPES OF GARDEN POTS

Pots are essential for a small space and can really change the look and feel of your garden. You can design them and adapt them to suit your aesthetics and really let your artistic side come into play. Or you can simply use them to move plants around the garden to benefit from sunlight and shade throughout the day.

The other thing to remember is that they don't simply have to be on the ground. You could hang your pots, attach them to your fences or have them on wooden ladders or book shelves on your balcony so that you maximize the space you have to grow in. It is all about getting creative. They are also a great way to keep adding to your garden.

Pots are really useful to grow plants such as mint that you need to contain or they will take over your whole garden. You will end up sifting through all your soil to make sure you have got all of the roots up like I once made the mistake of doing. Pots are also great for balconies, rooftops or even on canal boats where space is really limited.

RECYCLED MATERIALS

You can use anything to make a pot, from unloved plastic bottles to an old bucket that was used years ago to play on the beach. It is really important to use what we have to reduce wastage, reinventing how we use things in new and exciting ways. Just make sure you add holes to the base for drainage and think about how you will move them if they don't have a handle in their current form. You may also want to insulate them with a plastic bag.

CLAY OR TERRACOTTA POTS

They can look wonderful in a garden but they can be expensive and hard to move around a small space. If you drop them, they will crack rather than bounce and definitely hurt your toes. They are porous, which means water can easily escape and they dry out quicker than a plastic pot, but it does also mean that air can get into them. They are great if you are someone who has a tendency to over water plants!

The thick walls of the terracotta pot also acts as an insulator, which can help with temperature change and protecting plants. They are also useful to help with watering, as you can bury them to create your own DIY Olla (see page 165).

PLASTIC POTS

Plastic pots are easy to move around the garden and don't dry out as quickly as a clay or terracotta pot. You can often find them lying around or stacked up in people's gardens where they have bought plants from a nursery. They are great to grow seedlings in, to transplant in and to be able to move plants freely around your garden.

If you can help it, don't buy them new but try to use secondhand ones. Over 90 per cent of plastic pots are simply used to transport plants from point of sale to where they are planted, so there are lots out there.

 ## METAL POTS

Metal pots can look really cool and have a vintage, industrial feel about them. They are frost-proof and not too porous so they don't dry out like clay or terracotta. A big con though is their ability to control temperature. They heat up very quickly in the summer, and while they protect from frost, they can still get very cold in the winter. They can also corrode when left out all year, which makes them look unloved.

WOOD

Half whisky barrels are a great way to grow dwarf trees and other plants in your garden. You still have the luxury of moving them around or taking them with you without having to wait to transplant them when they are dormant if, like me, you have to move a lot as you are renting in a big city like London. I am always saying prevention is better than cure and it couldn't be more true here! It is a good idea to paint them with impermeable paint.

Half barrels can also be used to create great small ponds!

PRESERVING VEGETABLES

WHY SHOULD WE PRESERVE VEGETABLES?

Historically, preserving food was essential if anyone wanted to eat in the winter. Fresh food deteriorates quickly, especially in the heat of the summer. Even today, refrigerating food only slows down the inevitable, and freezing, while great for some things, like summer fruits, can destroy others – you're not going to want to freeze raw potatoes for example. If you are like me, you also only have a fixed amount of space in your freezer so it isn't possible to just put everything in there anyway.

When we grow our own produce, we often end up with gluts of fruit and veg that have ripened at the same time. This can mean that for a few weeks of the year you have so much of something you can't give it away fast enough, and you and everyone you know will soon get bored of it. I know I don't want any of my bountiful harvest to go to waste, so am always on the lookout for ways of preserving my homegrown food for as long as possible.

By using different methods of preserving food, you are not only able to preserve its flavour and nutritional value well out of season, but you will end up with a variety of tasty treats for your pantry or to give away as gifts. Receiving a couple of raw courgettes (zucchini) is nice, but if those courgettes have been roasted and preserved in oil for example, receiving a jar of delicious antipasto is certainly much nicer. What a treat to give your friends who have helped in your garden or donated recycled materials for your DIY builds.

PICKLING

Pickling is an ancient technique of preserving food in either vinegar or brine (salty water). It is relatively easy to do and the results can be delicious. In order for most bacteria and moulds to thrive they need food, water and oxygen. By taking one of these away you are making it very difficult for them to grow and therefore ruin food. That being said, the bacteria *Clostridium botulinum*, the cause of the potentially fatal botulism, does not need oxygen to survive, so it is important that we take away one of the others to preserve food safely.

As the food you are preserving is also the food for potential bacteria, we are not going to be able to take that away, and just removing the air isn't going to be enough. We need to do something about the water. Most bacteria is killed if subject to a pH level of 4.6 or lower, so that means that a sufficiently strong vinegar solution will be enough to kill most of the bacteria present. There is more that we can do to make it even safer though. There are three main types of pickling: quick pickling, salt brine and vinegar brine. I have shared how to do Giardiniera as an extra method, too.

QUICK PICKLING

Quick pickling is the simplest and (as the name implies) quickest way to pickle. However, it doesn't preserve the fruit or veg for a significant amount of time due to the presence of active water.

Vegetables such as cucumber, carrots and cauliflower, and fruits such as apples and cherries, are trimmed, sliced or left whole before either blanching, cooking or leaving raw, placed in a jar and covered in pickling liquid (1 part vinegar to 1 part water). Salt, sugar and aromatics (herbs and spices) can be added to taste.

Have fun experimenting with this and try different flavours. Don't worry if you get it wrong; you may also create something that tastes out of this world and this is how you learn. Leave your food pickling for an hour or two before serving, but it can last in a sterilized, sealed jar for a few weeks or up to a month depending on the food being pickled.

SALT BRINING

Salt brining is a technique that uses salt to draw out the natural moisture of fruit or veg, allowing it to be replaced by the vinegar. The prepared food is coated in either dry salt or left in a brine bath for at least a few hours, before being rinsed off and sealed into jars with a pickling liquid and aromatics. Salt and sugar can be added, not only affecting the taste and texture of the pickle, but by being dissolved in any water, so that bacteria can't grow.

VINEGAR BRINING

Vinegar brining is similar to salt brining, but the moisture is drawn out of the fruit or veg using vinegar rather than salt. This is done by repeatedly soaking the food in vinegar before draining it and soaking again. This can be quite a long process, but the results make for deliciously sharp and crunchy pickles. They are great to have to hand and can turn an ordinary meal into something rather extraordinary any day of the week. Gherkins are an excellent example of this method.

REDUCING THE RISK OF BACTERIAL GROWTH

- To further reduce the risk of bacterial growth, it is a good idea to pasteurize the pickling liquid before pouring it over the veg in sterilized jars. Simply heat the liquid to over 60°C (140°F) for five minutes.
- The simplest way to sterilize the clean jars is in an oven set to around 100°C (212°F) for five minutes. The lids can go in a pan of boiling water.
- Fill the sterilized jars while they are still hot and you will create a vacuum seal when you close the lid tightly. This will further aid the preservation of your pickle.
- Be careful when dealing with hot jars, lids and liquid. I would suggest you use tongs, oven gloves and jar funnels to make it as easy as possible.

ITALIAN QUICK PICKLING

Being an Italian, I've grown up with Giardiniera, a mix of pickled veg that we often call *sottaceti*. Here is a simple recipe for a fairly typical mix of veg, but feel free to mix it up and use what you have grown. It works brilliantly with courgettes, runner beans and if, like me, you like it a little spicy, chillies.

You will need:
- 1 litre (4 cups) cider or white wine vinegar
- 2–3 whole cloves
- 2–3 bay leaves
- ¼ tsp mustard seeds
- 1 tsp whole black peppercorns
- 1 tbsp salt
- 1 cauliflower, florets separated
- 8–10 pearl onions (or normal onions chopped into large chunks)
- 3–4 carrots, sliced into coins
- 2 celery sticks (stalks), cut into chunks (fennel is a great alternative)

1. Bring the vinegar to a rolling boil in a large pan and add the cloves, bay leaves, mustard seeds, peppercorns and salt.
2. Add the cauliflower, onions, carrots and celery to the vinegar and simmer for 10–15 minutes, until the veg is cooked, but still firm.
3. Use a slotted spoon to transfer the veg into a sterilized jam jar (see previous page).
4. Cover the veg with the vinegar and carefully seal the lid tightly while it's still very hot. This should create a vacuum seal.
5. Leave it in a cool, dark place for at least a few days, or up to a week. Once opened, eat within a week.

FERMENTING

Fermentation is the use of micro-organisms, such as yeast or bacteria, to change the nature of food through their metabolic process. These microorganisms convert starch or glucose into things like alcohol, lactic acid, acetic acid and carbon dioxide, which then limits bacterial growth.

The most famous type of fermentation is the use of yeast to convert the sugars found in grape, apple and barley into alcohol, which results in wine, cider and beer – something I definitely enjoy! This is done in an anaerobic environment (without oxygen), as the presence of oxygen will quickly convert the alcohol into aesthetic acid, or vinegar.

Another type of fermentation involving yeast that is not often thought of as such is baking bread. Yeast feeds on the dough and produces alcohol and carbon dioxide (yes, eating raw dough might get you drunk, although I don't recommend it). The alcohol completely evaporates when the bread is baked. Sourdough bread is more obviously a fermentation as the sourdough starter is made by fermenting flour in order to produce the carbon dioxide needed to make the bread rise.

Other fermentations that are popular are kefir, yogurt and even ice cream.

Fermented foods promote probiotics in your gut. These not only aid digestion, but can boost your immune system and even help with weight loss. Not only that, but fermented foods are easier for your gut to digest, and as they are usually made with raw vegetables, you are getting a massive boost of nutrients.

When fermenting vegetables, yeast is not required. Instead, an ideal environment is created for the right kind of bacteria to grow and eliminate any trace of potentially harmful bacteria. This is done by using salt to extract moisture from the vegetables, and then submerging them in brine without the presence of oxygen at a suitable temperature (18–22°C/64–71°F ideally).

The amount of salt used is quite important, as too little and fermentation may not occur, and the veg could go off. Too much could also stop fermentation, or taste too salty.

As a rule of thumb you should use 2–5 per cent salt, depending on the weight and density of the veg. A good number to start with is 2.2 per cent, which should yield good results every time. For example, if I have 100g (3½oz) cucumber, I will use a pinch of salt. If I have a more dense veg, like cauliflower, I might increase this slightly. You don't have to worry about being precise. You are not doing a chemistry exam; so long as there is enough salt to draw out the moisture and kill off unwanted bacteria (at least 2 per cent) you should be ok.

FERMENTING METHODS

There are two main techniques used when fermenting vegetables – when the vegetables are grated or shredded, as in kimchi or sauerkraut, and a dry salting method is used. Alternatively, if the vegetables are whole, or cut into chunks, then brine fermenting is used. In both cases, the salt ratio is the same.

Dry salting

Grated or shredded vegetables are coated in salt, which is then massaged in to help release the moisture. You then need to squeeze out a good quantity of liquid, which is a natural brine. Place the squeezed-out veg, along with any aromatics (garlic, chilli, herbs and spices), into a jar and cover with the natural brine.

Brine fermenting

The vegetables are put into a jar along with the aromatics and salt and then covered with water. This is then shaken up so the salt is dissolved.

With both techniques it is very important that all the veg is submerged below the water line. This is to eliminate the presence of oxygen, so that the bacteria can do its work and not spoil the product. It is advisable to use some kind of weight to keep the veg down. You can buy specialist jars and weights for this, but any glass jam jar and something small and heavy, like a stone, will do (just make sure that it's sterile before you put it in). The lid should be placed on, but not airtight, as CO_2 will be produced and you don't want it to explode.

The next step is to leave the jar of fermenting veg in a dark place between 18–22°C (64–71°F) for about three weeks. After this time all the necessary fermentation should have taken place. You can remove the weight, tighten the lid and transfer it to the refrigerator. The cold will slow down and stop any further fermentation from taking place.

Kombucha and SCOBY

SAUERKRAUT

One of the most famous fermented products is sauerkraut. It's absolutely delicious on pretty much anything and so simple to make. What is great is that it uses loads of cabbage, which once picked would otherwise go bad quite quickly, and is always too much to eat in one go. This dry salt method can of course be used to ferment a host of vegetables other than cabbage. Basically, if you can shred it, use it.

You will need:
- 1 cabbage, tough outer leaves and core removed
- Coarse sea salt
- 1 tsp caraway seeds
- 1 tsp black peppercorns

1. Place the cabbage in a large mixing bowl. Blanch the cabbage with boiling water, being careful that the bowl is big enough to fit the water in. (You don't want boiling water spilling all over you.)
2. Remove the cabbage from the water and use either a knife, mandolin or a food processor to shred it. The water can be discarded, or it makes an excellent base for stock.
3. Weigh the cabbage to work out how much salt you need. It should be between 2–5 per cent of the weight of the cabbage. If you don't have any scales, don't worry, the average cabbage will need about 3 tablespoons salt, but as I said earlier, you don't have to be exact.
4. Add the spices and massage the salt into the cabbage for about 5 minutes, then leave for a further five minutes. You should see a lot of brine start to come out of the cabbage, but you can give it a helping hand by squeezing it.
5. Put the cabbage with the spices into a sterilized jam jar and cover with the brine. Make sure all the cabbage is covered by brine. You may need to weigh it down to keep it submerged. Put the lid on, but don't close it tightly as you want the CO_2 to escape.
6. Leave in a dark place between 18–22°C (64–71°F) for at least five days, but preferably over two weeks. The longer you leave it, the more sour it will get, so taste it regularly. Check the fermentation every day and make sure you can see bubbles of CO_2 forming. Once these stop, the fermentation is completed. If you want to stop it sooner, put it in the refrigerator.
7. Screw on the lid tightly and store in the refrigerator for up to six months.

DEHYDRATING

Dehydrating fruit and veg is perhaps the simplest way to preserve them. In Italy, where I am from, we would simply leave all kinds of things outside in the sun to dry. In the heat of the Mediterranean summer everything would dry out in no time.

In the UK there may be a week in the height of summer where this is possible, but then you will have to keep your eyes on the skies looking for rain clouds. That being said, even on a cold, wet winter's day, drying produce is easy to do and needs little or no equipment to achieve great results.

As mentioned before, bacteria, like all life, need food, water and (usually) air to survive. By removing the moisture from any fruit or vegetable, you are making it impossible for bacteria to survive and therefore spoil the food. Dried food can last for years. In fact, there have been grains found in ancient Egyptian tombs that are over 5,000 years old that are not only still edible, but were germinated and grown into wheat.

Although not essential, a dehydrator is a great bit of kit to have in the kitchen. They can be bought in a range of prices and can often be found secondhand. Luckily, they are the kind of kitchen gadget often bought as a present, used once and then tidied away. Ask your friends and family and you might find that someone has one lurking in the back of a cupboard somewhere. Failing that, online selling platforms are likely to have them going cheaply, especially just after Christmas.

When choosing a dehydrator the most important feature for it to have is temperature control. Some of the cheaper ones are either on or off. This is probably fine for the majority of your drying needs, but if you want to dry more delicate things, such as edible flowers, basil leaves or wild garlic, then you will want them at a low temperature (50–60°C/122–140°F). More robust vegetables, or those with a higher water content, might need a higher temperature.

Another important feature to consider is a timer. Drying most things takes quite a while, so you tend to leave them to do their thing. Although they tend to be very energy efficient, you don't want them running unnecessarily.

If you don't have a dehydrator, or the space to keep one (they can be quite bulky), an oven works quite well. It helps if it's a fan-assisted oven as the airflow will take the moisture away from the food, but it isn't essential.

Most herbs and plenty of veg will dry nicely without a dehydrator or even an oven. Simply hanging them upside down in bunches will dry them out in a few days. Be sure to keep them out of sunlight, or they will get bleached and go a browny yellow colour.

Small fruit and veg, such as grapes or cherries and even plums, can often be left whole when dried. Larger, or more moist veg, such as tomatoes, might need to be cut in half or sliced thinly before drying. The thinner you slice the veg, the quicker it will dry and the crunchier it will get.

Most fruit and vegetables can be dehydrated, either raw or blanched/wilted first. The exception to this is potatoes.

Dried food can be rehydrated by soaking them in water (or stock or alcohol or whatever you want) when you want to use them, or they can be eaten or used dry, depending on the veg. Citrus fruits are a great example of this – they are perfect to dehydrate when in season in late winter to early spring and use throughout the rest of the year.

Top: Sauerkraut
Left: Dehydrating chillies

 EASY

INTERMEDIATE

ADVANCED

PART FOUR

TOP PLANTS FOR BEGINNERS

TOMATO (SOLANUM LYCOPERSICUM)

Tomatoes are one of my absolute favourites to grow and you can preserve them to enjoy all year round. I have beautiful memories of my grandpa's garden abundant with varieties and my grandma's kitchen with jars filled with flavoursome sauces.

Recommended cultivars/varieties: Crushed Heart, Zima, Chocolate Lightning, Tiger Stripe, Kryptonite, Cosmos, Black Beauty

Perennial or annual: Perennial

When to plant: Spring. Greenhouse: Sow them from late February to mid-March Outside: March to early April.

Where to plant: In direct sunlight. They grow well with Basil and Calendula.

Size: 1–3m (3–10ft) in height

How to grow: Choose determinate (bush) or indeterminate (vine) varieties. Determinants are bushy and will grow well without support in pots. Indeterminates will grow better from the ground or grow bags and will need canes, tripods or a trellis to support them.

You can save the seeds of your favourite tomatoes. Slice open a ripe tomato and scoop out the gelatin (which acts as a sprout inhibitor) and

seeds into a cup. Mix daily to prevent mould for two to three days. Once your seeds have sunk to the bottom leave them to dry and store them in a labelled paper bag ready to use next season. Store-bought tomatoes are normally indeterminate.

Germinate the seeds in early spring if you have a propagator, or late spring on the windowsill. Fill a seed tray or small pots with moist compost and sow two or three seeds per pot. Cover with a clear plastic sheet (clingfilm/plastic wrap) or bowl and leave in a warm place (18°C/64°F).

When you start getting saplings, remove the plastic and keep them in direct sunlight for about two weeks, or until they are big enough to repot. You can move or replant them outside when the threat of frost has gone.

Water regularly and feed with tomato feed once a week. With vine types, you will want to use a cane as support and nip off any side shoots as they appear.

How to feed: High potash tomato feed once a week.

Common diseases and pests: Blossom end rot – you will notice dark blotches on the ends. Make sure you keep the soil moist by watering regularly to prevent it. Tomato blight – occurs in wet weather – choose a variety that is resistant to this and have good drainage in place.

Tomato leaf mould – yellow blotches on the leaves – this normally happens when grown in a greenhouse due to poor ventilation.

Cracking or splitting – thankfully this won't change the taste but it leaves it open to fungus or mould. To avoid this water regularly and if in a greenhouse monitor temperature.

How to harvest: Harvest tomatoes when they are completely red if possible, but they will continue to ripen after being picked.

CUCUMBER *(CUCUMIS SATIVUS)*

Cucumbers are the perfect summer staple, being 95 per cent water and packed with vitamins and minerals. Not only are they a thirst quencher, they are really healthy too.

Recommended cultivars/varieties: Pony, Crystal Lemon, White Wonder, Kiwano

Perennial or annual: Annual

When to plant: Start sowing seeds in late winter/early spring and plant out in late spring/early summer.

Where to plant: There are two types of cucumber: outdoor or greenhouse. Greenhouse varieties need a lot of space and heat and will produce the kind of cucumbers you see in the supermarket. Outdoor cucumbers like a sunny, sheltered spot and will produce shorter, fatter fruit. It is important to know the difference, because if you plant outdoor varieties next to indoor ones you risk cross pollination, resulting in bitter, seedy fruit.

Size: Up to 2m (6½ft)

How to grow: Start sowing seeds in small pots with multipurpose compost from late winter if you have a propagator or heated greenhouse, or early spring on a sunny windowsill. You will want them to be at around 20°C (70°F) to germinate. Make sure that the seeds are pointing upward.

When you start seeing proper leaves coming through (about three weeks), it is time to repot them. If you are using greenhouse varieties, you can put them in there in mid-spring. Plant outside varieties after the threat of frost has gone. Both varieties like nutritious compost and can be fed with tomato feed fortnightly.

Greenhouse cucumbers can be grown up canes or frames and you will want to pinch off side shoots and tips when they start getting too tall. Outdoor varieties will tend to sprawl across the ground but you can attach the main stem to a wire mesh or trellis, and train the side shoots up the trellis as well.

Greenhouse varieties like humid conditions (spray a fine water mist on them) and both like to be watered little and often. Once they start to flower you can feed them once a week.

Some varieties of greenhouse cucumber need to have the male flowers removed to prevent pollination. If the flower has a small cucumber behind it, then it is female, so leave it, but if not it is male, so pinch it off. For outdoor varieties, both male and female flowers are needed.

Cucumbers

How to feed: Use plant feed high in potash.

Common diseases and pests: Cucumber mosaic virus is a common disease that is caused by aphids. You will see a yellow, mosaic pattern on the leaves. Unfortunately there is no cure, so if you see it, get rid of the plant to stop it from spreading.

How to harvest: The size of a ripe cucumber very much depends on the variety, but it is better to pick them early than late as they can grow thick skinned and bitter. Use a sharp knife or secateurs to cut them from the stem. The more you harvest the more they will produce.

COURGETTE/ZUCCHINI (CUCURBITA PEPO)

As an Italian, I have a special place in my heart for this wonderful vegetable.

Recommended cultivars/varieties:
Golden Courgette, Green Bush, Striped Courgette

Perennial or annual: Annual

When to plant: Sow seeds indoors in spring and young plants outside in summer .

Where to plant: Grow in a sunny spot, leaving about 1m (3ft) around it to grow.

Size: Courgette plants can grow to about 1m (3ft) in diameter and the fruit should be harvested when it reaches around 10–12cm (4–5in).

How to grow: Plant one or two seeds in small pots filled with warm compost and water thoroughly. You want to keep the temperature around 20°C (68°F) so that they germinate well. Once seedlings have started popping up, select the biggest, strongest ones and move them to bigger pots. Keep them indoors until late spring/early summer (after the risk of frost has gone).

When you plant them outside, make sure you leave plenty of space for them to grow. You will want to use plenty of compost. The soil should be kept moist but not soggy and it is a good idea to feed them regularly. I like to use tomato food once every couple of weeks or so.

How to feed: High potash plant food

Common diseases and pests:
Young plants are a favourite of slugs and snails. Use crushed eggshells around the plant to help keep them away.

If the conditions are too dry, the plant will only grow male flowers, which will not produce fruit. If it's too wet, you might get rotten fruit. Keep the soil nice and moist by watering the base of the plant, not the leaves and using mulch to retain moisture. If you notice a rotting leaf, pick it off before the rot spreads.

How to harvest: Cut the courgette at the base with a sharp knife when it is about 10cm (4in) long.

AUBERGINE/EGGPLANT (SOLANUM MELONGENA)

Aubergines are so versatile; they can be used in anything from curries to baba ganoush, or are delicious simply sliced, salted and barbecued.

Recommended cultivars/varieties:
Violetta di Firenze

Perennial or annual: Annual

When to plant: If you have a heated propagator or airing cupboard, sow seeds in winter, if not early spring. Plant out in early summer after the threat of frost.

Where to plant: Aubergines like a lot of sun and moist soil, often doing best in a greenhouse. If you don't have a greenhouse, choose a warm sunny, south-facing spot that is out of the wind.

Size: Can grow at least 90cm (3ft) tall

How to grow: Aubergines take a long time to grow, so get planting early. Plant the seeds in well watered, peat-free compost and keep in a heated propagator or airing cupboard for about three weeks, or until the first leaves start to appear. At this point, repot and move to a warm and sunny windowsill or greenhouse.

Once the threat of frost has passed they can be moved outside and repotted or planted directly in the ground, although if you have space in a greenhouse, you might want to keep them in there. They will benefit from growing against a frame or cane, much like their cousin, the tomato. You might need to tap the flowers as they grow to release the pollen, especially if growing in a greenhouse, away from pollinators. You will also want to pinch away any growing tips to encourage side shoots to grow.

How to feed: Feed weekly with high potash fertilizer such as tomato feed.

Common diseases and pests: The most common challenge with aubergines is insect pests such as aphids. The best defence against these are ladybirds, which you can get online.

Blossom end rot is a result of a lack of calcium, causing the cells to collapse and a bruise to appear on the tip of the fruit. Make sure that your plant is well watered and has rich compost. Tomato feed will also help to prevent this problem.

How to harvest: Pluck the fruit when it is still shiny as it will lose its gloss as it becomes overripe.

CHILLIES (CAPSICUM FRUTESCENS)

It was chillies that got me into growing and remains my favourite thing to grow. There is something for everyone: from sweet "Tangerine" chilli to the infamous Naga.

Recommended cultivars/varieties:
Black Gold

Perennial or annual: Annual

When to plant: Sow seeds as early as January if you have a heated propagator, or in March on a sunny windowsill.

Plant in a greenhouse in May or late May/June if doing so outdoors.

Where to plant: Chillies like the sun so if you don't have a greenhouse, choose a sunny, sheltered spot, preferably south facing.

Size: A vine type chilli can grow up to about 3m (10ft) tall, depending on variety and conditions. A bush type can grow to 2m (6½ft) but will be limited by the size of pot they are grown in (if any).

How to grow: If you are lucky enough to have a heated propagator and growing lights, then sow your seeds in mid-winter in multi-purpose compost. If you don't, then a sunny windowsill in early spring works really well. Keep the soil moist and warm.

Repot as soon as you see some proper leaves. If you are growing a bushy variety then you can put them straight into their final pot. Otherwise, you might want to keep repotting in increasingly bigger pots as they grow.

Plant in a greenhouse in late spring, or outside early summer. Start feeding with tomato feed weekly as soon as you start seeing flowers. Vine varieties will benefit from growing up a cane or trellis, and you will want to pinch out growing tips to encourage a more bushy plant.

If you want really hot chillies grow them in a hot environment; I would recommend a greenhouse. Stop feeding them as soon as fruit starts to appear and water much less. If you let the soil dry out completely this will stress the plant and make the chillies hotter, but you will get a smaller crop.

How to feed: Use plant feed high in potash.

Chillies

Common diseases and pests: Blossom end rot is a result of a lack of calcium, causing the cells to collapse and a bruise to appear on the tip of the fruit. Make sure that your plant is well watered and has rich compost. Tomato feed will also help to prevent this problem.

Grey mould can appear on over-crowded plants that don't get much ventilation. Ensure that the plant has room to grow and good airflow and if any mould should appear, remove it immediately.

How to harvest: The chillies should be ready to harvest in midsummer. Pick them when they are green if you want a milder, more zingy flavour, or when red for more heat. They will also ripen once picked if left in the sun.

RADISH (RAPHANUS SATIVUS)

I love radishes as they are so quick and easy to grow and add a delicious, peppery flavour to salads and sandwiches.

Recommended cultivars/varieties: White Icicle, Round Black Spanish

Perennial or annual: Annual

When to plant: Sow early crops in succession (small batches at regular intervals) from late winter. Sow main crops from spring right through to late summer.

For winter varieties, start sowing in succession in mid to late summer.

Where to plant: Radishes prefer direct sun, but will do well in partial shade. They are great when planted in between other, slower growing crops, like potatoes, as they will suppress weeds and can act as a border line.

Size: 15cm (6in)

How to grow: With both winter and summer varieties available, succession planting allows you to have fresh radish growing all year round. Start sowing seeds directly into the ground from late winter, using fleeces and cloches to keep them warm. Plant the seeds about 1cm (⅓in) deep and about 2.5cm (1in) appart. Water regularly and thin out if necessary.

Common diseases and pests: Young plants are a favourite of slugs and snails. Use crushed eggshells around the plant to help keep them away.

How to harvest: Young leaves are great in salads and as a garnish. Bear this in mind when thinning.

Radishes

CORN (ZEA MAYS)

Nothing looks better than a few tall corn plants wafting in a summer breeze in your garden. And as a bonus, you get delicious corn on the cob too!

Recommended cultivars/varieties: Glass Gem corn, Strawberry corn

Perennial or annual: Annual

When to plant: Late spring, early summer

Where to plant: In full sun. Great at providing shade and shelter for ground crops such as cucumber, squash or potatoes.

Size: 2m (6½ft)

How to grow: Sow seeds indoors in late spring either in a propagator or on a warm windowsill. Use deep pots covering the seeds with 2.5cm (1in) of compost. They need to be kept at around 18–21°C (65–70°F) to germinate. This can be done in succession, with different varieties to ensure an extended cropping time.

You might want to add high potassium fertilizer to the compost before planting. When frost has passed, plant in sunlight in blocks rather than rows. This is because they are wind pollinated. You can assist by tapping the top of male flowers.

How to feed: Dig high potassium fertilizer into the soil if necessary.

Common diseases and pests: Sweetcorn can attract birds, rodents, slugs and snails. Netting can protect from these.

How to harvest: Cobs are ready to harvest by midsummer, when the stringy bits have turned brown. Test it by piercing a kernel with your fingernail. If the liquid that comes out is milky, it is ripe.

BEETROOT/BEET *(BETA VULGARIS)*

The deep pink colour of beetroot is like no other. You can even eat every part of this wonderful plant. Early American settlers used it to make pink icing for cakes!

Recommended cultivars/varieties:
Rainbow beetroot, Sugar Beets

Perennial or annual: Annual

When to plant: Spring to summer

Where to plant: They grow best in full sun but can take some light shade. They like moist soil and can be grown in raised beds and pots too.

Size: The size of a golf ball to tennis ball

How to grow: To make sure you have a constant supply throughout the late summer and autumn, sow in weekly intervals from early spring.

You can sow the seeds directly into moist soil. You will need to thin your crop once they are 2.5c (1in) high to leave a space of 4cm (10in) apart.

Common diseases and pests: The most common problem is bolting. To stop this, use varieties that are less likely to bolt and don't let them dry out. So make sure you water them in dry spells but be careful not to overwater.

How to harvest: Pull back some of the soil and see if you can see the round bulb pushing up through the soil. This is a sure sign they are ready. Simply twist and pull on the leaves to harvest. Don't leave them in the ground for too long – they will continue to grow, especially in summer months, but they will become woody to taste.

CARROT (DAUCUS CAROTA)

You simply can't beat the flavour of homegrown carrots. It's amazing to think they started off purple until the Dutch developed the mutant orange strain.

Recommended cultivars/varieties: Cosmic, Rainbow Mix

Perennial or annual: Annual (if left out for a second year, the carrots will turn bitter)

When to plant: Spring and summer

Where to plant: They thrive in sunshine and like soil that drains easily. So remove as many weeds and stones as you can before you plant. You can also grow them in pots and you get a lot of produce for a small space due to their size. Just make sure the pot is deep enough to hold them.

They thrive next to alliums including chives and garlic which help to protect them from carrot fly.

Size: 5–50cm (2–20in)

How to grow: You can sow seeds directly into the soil. Make a 1cm (⅓in) deep trench and plant them about 5cm (2in) apart. Cover them with soil and water.

You can sow them at two week intervals for a longer harvest time and also use varieties that crop at different times. Be careful not to crush the tops as the smell attracts carrot fly.

Common diseases and pests: Carrot fly – a small black fly whose larvae feast on the roots of the carrot. There isn't much you can do once they arrive so prevention is key! Plant them with companion plants like chives and garlic to mask the smell, and plant them in groups rather than all your carrots together.

Aphids – this greenfly likes the leaves of the plant. Ladybirds love aphids – so buy ladybirds and let nature do its job.

How to harvest: Carrots are normally ready 12–16 weeks after planting. Pull a few carrots to see if they are ready. You can leave them in the ground to store. Don't forget you can eat the carrot tops – they are great in a pesto!

CHARD (BETA VULGARIS)

Chard is easy to grow and you can harvest it all year round, meaning you have a ready supply of a delicious fresh veg straight to your kitchen table!

Recommended cultivars/varieties:
Rainbow chard

Perennial or annual: Biannual

When to plant: Spring/summer

Where to plant: In sun or partial sun. Works well under sweetcorn.

Size: Up to 60cm (2ft)

How to grow: You can sow directly into the ground. You have a choice of planting twice – spring and midsummer to get a constant supply – or choosing a cut-and-come-again crop. To sow them make a 2.5cm (1in) deep trench and place them 4cm (1½in) apart. Water and add some mulch to protect the seedlings.

You can harvest them until the plant no longer produces leaves or tastes good.

Common diseases and pests: Birds, especially pigeons, love to come and feast. You can cover with netting or you could use a scarecrow – make sure you move it around as the birds soon get used to them.

Grey mould – this normally starts off as a discoloured patch and can spread, so you want to remove it as quickly as possible. It can survive over winter as a black resting spore. It normally appears in damp or humid conditions. Check on your chard more often in these conditions and remove it as quickly as possible.

Downy mildew – you will see this on the leaves. The best way is to prevent it by not planting too close together so there is room for air to circulate, choosing varieties that are less prone to it and watering the soil at the base.

How to harvest: Use the young leaves raw in a salad and mature ones cooked like spinach. Start with the outer leaves and work toward the middle so you get regrowth and a constant supply. This is a great one to swap with friends.

LETTUCE (LACTUCA SATIVA)

Lettuce grown at home is packed full of flavour and it is perfect for beginners to grow as it is easy and gives quick results.

Recommended cultivars/varieties: Lolla Rossa, Cosmic Crimson

Perennial or annual: Annual

When to plant: From spring to early autumn

Where to plant: Lettuce likes direct sun, sheltered from the wind.

Size: 30–100cm (12–40in) in height

How to grow: Sow seeds directly into the ground, growbag or pots in direct sunlight, keeping the soil moist. You will want to grow a few plants at a time in succession, so that you have a continuous supply. Early and late sown seeds may need to be protected from frost. You can do this with a fleece, cloches or a plastic tunnel.

Sow seeds in rows about 30cm (12in) apart, with a thin layer of soil over them, about 1cm (⅓in) and water generously. As the seeds start to germinate and grow, thin them out by picking out the weaklings, until you have strong plants about 30cm (12in) apart.

Common diseases and pests: Birds like sparrows and pigeons love lettuce. You might want to cover the plants with fleece or chicken wire, or maybe use a scarecrow.

How to harvest: Harvest when the lettuce looks like it's worth eating. Use a sharp knife to cut it away from the stem close to the ground.

Rainbow Lettuce

PUMPKIN *(CUCURBITA)*

Pumpkins aren't just for halloween; they're great to eat in pies, soups, risotto, roasted or in vegetable curries.

Recommended cultivars/varieties: Butternut squash. For those short on space, Jack Be Little pumpkins are great miniatures that make fantastic halloween decorations, as well as tasting brilliant.

Perennial or annual: Annual

When to plant: Spring/early summer

Where to plant: Choose a sunny, sheltered spot out of the wind. Most pumpkin varieties need plenty of space too.

Size: Around 1.2–2.5m (4–8ft) spread, depending on variety. Can grow enormous.

How to grow: Sow seeds indoors in early spring, or early summer outdoors, making sure that the seed is on its side and under about 1cm (⅓in) of compost. Water well.

If you are growing them indoors, you will want to get them used to being outside in late spring, by putting them out during the day, and bringing them back in again at night. Do this for about a week before planting them in early June.

You will want to water the plant a lot, but make sure that it drains away. Once you start getting fruit, you might want to put it on a tile or some glass to keep it off the ground and prevent it from rotting.

Common diseases and pests: Leaves can get a powdery mildew if it's too hot and wet. Keep soil nice and moist, but not waterlogged.

How to harvest: Harvest before the first frost (about halloween time) using a sharp knife to cut the stem.

Pumpkin

SPRING ONION/SCALLION (ALLIUM FISTULOSUM)

Spring onions are so easy to grow, you can be harvesting them directly from your windowsill in no time.

Recommended cultivars/varieties: Lilia

Perennial or annual: Annual

When to plant: Spring to summer

Where to plant: Sunny, sheltered spot. They do well on a south-facing windowsill.

Size: Up to 30cm (12in)

How to grow: Seeds can be sown directly into the ground or in containers. Use a rake or a stick to create a shallow trench, around 1cm (⅓in) deep and thinly sprinkle your seeds in before covering with soil and water well. You might want to put something like a fleece over them to stop the birds from getting to them and to keep them warm if sowing early or late.

Keep the soil moist, but not overwatered, and make sure the area is weed-free. If growing in pots, you will want to water a bit more often. Grow new seeds every three weeks or so to ensure you have a constant supply.

Common diseases and pests: Onion white rot can be spread from other affected alliums, or from the soil where they have been previously, so it's best to rotate the location of your alliums, as once they have it, there is not much you can do.

Downy mildew can appear if the onions are too wet. Avoid overwatering, and make sure that there is good drainage and air circulation. If it should appear, pick off the affected leaves.

How to harvest: Pick your spring onions as you need them from about eight weeks after sowing. They should be about 15cm (6in) tall and still young and tender looking.

Spring Onions

LEEK (ALLIUM PORRUM)

Leeks are a fantastic winter crop that is so easy to grow, and absolutely delicious when covered in cheese sauce with your Christmas dinner.

Recommended cultivars/varieties:
Northern Light, Blue Solaise

Perennial or annual: Annual

When to plant: Autumn/winter

Where to plant: Sunny spot

Size: 45cm (18in)

How to grow: Seeds can be sown directly into the ground or in containers. Use a rake or a stick to create a shallow trench 1.5cm (½in) deep and thinly sprinkle your seeds in before covering with soil, and water well. You might want to put something like a fleece over them to stop the birds from getting to them and to keep them warm.

Keep the soil moist, but not overwatered, and make sure the area is weed-free. If growing in pots, water more often. You can increase the size of the white part of the leek by wrapping it in newspaper to block out the light. Don't be tempted to use soil here, as it'll get in the leek and make it difficult to clean.

Common diseases and pests: Onion white rot can be spread from other affected alliums, or from the soil where they have been previously, so it's best to rotate the location of your alliums, as once they have it, there is not much you can do.

Downy mildew can appear if the leeks are too wet. Avoid overwatering, and make sure that there is good drainage and air circulation. If it should appear, pick off the affected leaves.

How to harvest: Once the leek is big enough (this is up to you really as you can pick them as baby leeks if you want), simply tug them out of the ground. You might need to use a garden fork to help. Leeks will stay in the ground for as long as you need them.

Leeks

ONIONS (ALLIUM CEPA)

The onion is the most widely used vegetable in the world, being the base of almost every dish from every cuisine across the globe. This might be because they are so versatile, and easy to grow and store.

Recommended cultivars/varieties: Tosca, Bedfordshire Champion

Perennial or annual: Annual

When to plant: Winter/spring/autumn

Where to plant: Onions need full sun. It's a good idea to plant alongside parsley to ward off onion fly.

Size: Depending on the variety, onions can grow from the size of a ping-pong ball to the size of a small soccer ball.

How to grow: You can grow onions either from seed, or from sets, which are basically small onions. If growing from seed, sow them indoors as early as mid-winter. You will want to plant the seeds in compost about 1cm (⅓in) apart and water well. Once you have a decent seedling you will want to replant them about 10–15cm (4–6in) apart, keeping them indoors until the spring.

Plant sets out in the spring or autumn in a sunny spot, about 10–15cm (4–6in) apart and keep moist and weed-free.

Common diseases and pests: Onion fly can be avoided by planting parsley nearby.

Onion neck rot can be a problem if overwatered. Make sure that the soil has good drainage and they are not overcrowded.

How to harvest: Harvest using a garden fork when the onions are big enough or the leaves have started to wilt. They will need to be left to dry on newspaper (turning occasionally) or a drying rack for two to three weeks before being stored by hanging them from string in a cool, dark place.

SPINACH (SPINACIA OLERACEA)

Spinach is fantastic to grow as it's the plant that keeps on giving. Cut young leaves for salads, wilting the more mature ones, and it will keep growing more.

Perennial or annual: Annual

When to plant: Winter/spring/summer/autumn

Where to plant: Partial shade. Grows very well under sweetcorn.

Size: 30cm (12in)

How to grow: Dig a small trench, about 1.5cm (½in) deep in good, moist compost in partial shade and sprinkle in the seeds. Keep rows about 40cm (15in) apart. Cover in soil and water well. Thin out as necessary.

Do this once or twice a month except at the height of summer, and you should have a good crop of spinach all year round.

Common diseases and pests: Spinach is susceptible to slugs and snails, so use crushed up eggshells to make it difficult for them.

Mildew is another problem, especially in humid weather. Make sure the plants have plenty of space for air circulation and try to avoid watering the leaves.

How to harvest: You can start harvesting leaves from about six weeks; just pick the ones that look the best and the plant will keep growing more.

PEAS (PISUM SATIVUM)

There is nothing like the taste of fresh peas straight from the pod, and they're so beautiful when in flower that they will make any growing space look amazing.

Recommended cultivars/varieties: Purple Mange Tout, Carouby de Mausamme

Perennial or annual: Annual

When to plant: Spring/summer

Where to plant: Full sun in pots or directly in the ground up canes or a trellis.

Size: 1.2–1.8m (4–6ft) tall

How to grow: Sow seeds directly into the ground from spring to early summer by digging a trench about 20cm (8in) wide and 3cm (1in) deep in a warm, sunny spot. Place each seed 10cm (4in) apart and cover with soil before watering well.

Pea plants will need something to climb up as they grow, so use a thin cane, a trellis or even some netting while they are still small and train them to climb up high.

Common diseases and pests: Pea moth larvae can be a problem, especially for young plants. Covering them with something like a fleece should help.

Slugs and snails, birds and rodents will also like to eat your pea plants. The fleece will help with this, or you could try surrounding the plants with netting.

How to harvest: If your variety is more like a mange tout (snow peas) then you will want to harvest them as soon as you see the first signs of peas developing. Otherwise, wait until they are bursting out of their pods before simply picking each pod from the plant.

Peas

BEANS (PHASEOLUS VULGARIS)

Not only are beans delicious and nutritious, they are also easy to grow and make a fantastic, beautiful border plant.

Recommended cultivars/varieties: Trinity, and for more experienced, confident gardeners, Snake Beans

Perennial or annual: Annual

When to plant: Spring/summer

Where to plant: Full sun. Great as a decorative border and for giving shade to things like spinach.

Size: 3–4m (10–13ft) tall

How to grow: Start sowing your seeds indoors in early spring. You will want to use deep pots, or even an old toilet roll tube to develop strong roots. Plant out after the threat of frost has passed in late spring/early summer. Find a sunny spot, and remember that the plants will need support to grow, something like a trellis or a wigwam would be perfect.

Plant them at the base of the canes or trellis 20cm (8in) apart, tie on the shoots as they grow and keep the ground moist.

Common diseases and pests: Slugs and snails are a common problem for beans. Either use eggshells to deter them, or some other gritty substance, like gravel.

How to harvest: Pick regularly from about 12 weeks, or when the beans are about 15–20cm (6–7in) long. Regular harvesting will encourage more growth.

Beans

POTATOES (SOLANUM TUBEROSUM)

What's not to love about potatoes, and there is nothing quite like homegrown new potatoes, freshly harvested from your own growing space.

Recommended cultivars/varieties: Congo Blue, Blue Ammelise, Allouette

Perennial or annual: Annual

When to plant: Spring

Where to plant: Sunny spot out of the wind. Avoid areas prone to a late frost.

Size: Up to 1m (3¼ft) tall

How to grow: New potatoes (first or second earlies) grow well in containers. You can buy special potato growing bags, but just about anything will do, so long as it has plenty of drainage. An Ikea bag with holes cut into the bottom works perfectly.

Fill the bag about a third of the way up with some rich compost and place in one or two seed potatoes: this is a potato that has started to sprout (if you use two you will get more, slightly smaller, potatoes). Cover this with compost and water well. You will want to keep the compost moist at all times, and out of a cold wind.

As the plant grows, cover the shoot with more compost. Repeat this until the bag is full. This will give the root system room to grow and maximize your harvest.

Once the bag is full, keep the compost moist until your potatoes are ready to harvest.

Common diseases and pests: Potato blight is a common fungal infection that is caused by warm, wet weather. It first appears as dark splodges on the leaves, and can soon destroy entire crops. Make sure that you have good drainage and that the compost is never waterlogged. If you spot the blight early, you can cut all the foliage away to prevent it from affecting the potatoes.

How to harvest: Ready to harvest in midsummer, when there are still flowers on the plants. Simply tip the container out and root through the compost for your potatoes.

GINGER (ZINGIBER OFFICINALE)

This fantastic vegetable/spice has such a great flavour, both in cooking and as a tea, and is so easy to grow at home you will wonder why you ever bought it from the store.

Perennial or annual: Perennial

When to plant: Spring

Where to plant: Indoors or in pots outside in full sun (UK) or partial shade (hot climates).

Size: 30cm (12in)

How to grow: Buy some good quality root ginger from your local supermarket, making sure that it has at least two "eyes" on it, then bury it in a little compost with the eyes poking out. keep it warm and moist for a few weeks or until shoots start to develop. Repot into a large pot, and keep covering the stem as it grows, watering generously.

In the summer the pots can live outside in full sunshine, unless it's too hot, then move to the shade. Bring them in before the first frost.

Common diseases and pests: Ginger is resistant to most diseases, but if they are in an overcrowded greenhouse, you might get glasshouse red spider mite. To prevent this, keep the greenhouse humid by spraying water mist regularly.

How to harvest: When the plant stops producing leaves in the autumn you can dig up the root and cut away part of it, leaving the rest to grow next year.

CABBAGE (BRASSICA OLERACEA)

Cabbage is amazingly versatile and often gets overlooked! It's great chopped up raw in a summer slaw, roasted, braised, or even grilled. They can be surprisingly pretty too!

Perennial or annual: Annual

When to plant: Spring to late summer

Where to plant: A sunny spot with firm soil – which is soil you don't sink into as you walk across it. Cabbages are happiest in the ground but you can grow them individually as long as you use a deep pot.

Size: Can grow to the size of a football. (One couple in Australia grew one to the size of a person!)

How to grow: It's important to think about space when growing cabbages. Sow directly into the ground with a thin layer of seeds or start from seed indoors six to eight weeks before the last frost. Then you can transplant them outside.

Cabbages love water! So make sure you use the puddle technique: move them after rain or fill the hole for your cabbages with water the night before you move them and then water again when you pop them into their new home.

You can succession plant to ensure you have a good supply. They take between 4–6 months to be ready to harvest.

Common diseases and pests: Caterpillars love them, with cabbage white butterflies being the most common. Put netting over them or if you see them you can pick them off.

Club root can occur when drainage isn't good or if the soil is too alkaline. You will notice the leaves become pale yellow and wilt. To avoid this make sure you have good drainage and you can add some lime to the soil.

Slugs and snails love cabbage. Their snail trail will announce their arrival. A great natural way to keep them away is coffee grounds or eggs shells.

Cabbage

TOMATILLO (PHYSALIS PHILADELPHICA)

Tomatillos have a beautifully tart flavour and are the key ingredient for a Mexican salsa. They make my mouth water when I think of them chopped up with chilli and coriander, drizzled with lime and seasoned with salt. Perfect outside on a warm September evening.

Recommended cultivars/varieties:
Purple tomatillo

Perennial or annual: Perennial, but grown as annual

When to plant: Summer

Where to plant: They love the sun and an area with good drainage. You can grow them in a pot in a nice sunny spot and they produce a great yield.

Size: They are quite bushy and grow to be 0.5–1m (2–3ft) feet tall.

How to grow: You need to plant two plants or they will not pollinate as they are sterile. Sterile means that the flowers of an individual plant will not pollinate themselves. The yield is prolific, so two or three plants should be more than enough!

You can sow them inside, six to eight weeks before the last expected frost.

Their fruit can weigh them down so I would recommend staking, using a trellis or caging them to support them like you would tomatoes.

Common diseases and pests: Aphids – these black flies can take over, but the best way to control them is by introducing ladybirds to feast on them.

How to harvest: You can pick them off once the fruit is nice and firm and the husk is dry and is the right colour for the variety you have chosen.

Tomatillo

CELERY *(APIUM GRAVEOLENS)*

Celery is something I always have in my garden as part of the "holy trinity" in Italian cooking. Soffritto is used as a base in many dishes: chopped carrot, celery and onion.

Recommended cultivars/varieties:
Pink celery

Perennial or annual: Annual

When to plant: Spring

Where to plant: A sunny and moist area. Nasturtiums and marigolds are great companions to keep pests away.

Size: 45–60cm (18–20in)

How to grow: Thinly sow the seeds and cover with a thin layer of compost. They are ready to pot when they have a few leaves that are easy to handle. Be careful that the temperature doesn't drop too low as it can cause them to bolt later, compromising their otherwise great taste.

Alternatively you can harden them off and plant them in trenches outside. One of the most important things is to ensure they never dry out. Wild celery loves to be in wet conditions.

Common diseases and pests: Slugs and snails love to snack on the young plant. Their snail trail will announce their arrival. Keep them away with coffee grounds or eggs shells.

Powdery mildew which looks like someone has powdered the leaves! Make sure your plant has enough water and good air circulation. It is most likely to occur as the weather warms up in early spring. Pluck the infected leaves and thin the plants if needed for better circulation.

How to harvest: It is important to blanch celery before you harvest it. Cover the stems for two to three weeks before harvesting. Celery takes 18–20 weeks to mature so make a note! If you don't, your celery will become too bitter. To harvest, cut at the base with a knife. Pop your harvested celery in water on a windowsill. It is amazing how long it can last!

Celery

GLOBE ARTICHOKE (CYNARA SCOLYMUS)

Globe artichokes are both stunning in the garden with their alien-like displays and are delicious cooked simply in butter in the kitchen.

Perennial or annual: Perennial

When to plant: Spring/summer

Where to plant: They like a warm, sunny spot in an area with good drainage.

Size: Up to 1m (3ft)

How to grow: Start them off inside in seed trays, and once they have five leaves you can transport them out into the garden. They can be planted in your flower borders or in your veg patch. They do grow quite big and need space to spread out bear this in mind when planting.

If you have a friend who has some, ask them to divide their plant for you if it is a few years old. It will benefit them as they will produce more and you will quickly have a well established plant.

Be sure to water well and keep weed-free.

Common diseases and pests: Slugs and snails love to snack on the young plant. Watch for snail trails. A great natural way to keep them away is coffee grounds or eggs shells.

They attract aphids too; the best remedy is buying some ladybirds to feast upon them, controlling your garden naturally.

How to harvest: Use secateurs to harvest them when they reach the size of a golf ball. You will be rewarded as you will get more than one flower bud. They are so tasty.

Globe Artichoke

FENNEL (FOENICULUM VULGARE)

Fennel grows wild across Italy and you can smell its slightly aniseed fragrance through the air. It is a delight to have in the kitchen as you can eat all of it from its stalk to fronds to its seeds and it definitely deserves a spot at your dinner table.

Recommended cultivars/varieties: Bronze fennel

Perennial or annual: Perennial

When to plant: Late spring/summer

Where to plant: A sheltered, sunny spot. It grows well in pots and this can be a helpful way to grow it to stop cross contamination.

Size: 1–1.2m (3–4ft) tall

How to grow: You can sow fennel inside but be careful not to disturb the root ball when you transplant it. It is much better to sow your seeds directly in your veg patch after the last frost.

Fennel is low maintenance and once it is established is pretty drought-resilient. You will need to remove the dead stems but the rest of the plant will die down naturally in autumn. Which is one less thing for you to think about!

Common diseases and pests: Powdery mildew, which looks like someone has powdered the leaves! Make sure your plant has enough water and circulation. It is most likely to occur as the weather warms up in early spring. So pluck the infected leaves and thin the plant if needed for better circulation.

Aphids make their homes under the leaves and can be a real pain. A great way to control them is to introduce ladybirds or lacewings to your garden.

How to harvest: You can start using the leaves once established, but only take a few at a time so you don't kill the plant. The bulb is ready once it reaches the size of a tennis ball. Check this by uncovering the earth around it to see. You can also harvest the seeds for cooking and to share with friends!

Fennel

MUSHROOMS (AGARICUS BISPORUS)

Growing your own mushroom is an amazing way to maximize food production, especially if you own a small growing space like my urban garden here in London. It is also an excellent way to help your plants thrive much better by improving their water and nutrient absorption thanks to a few varieties of mushrooms like wine caps.

Perennial or annual: Perennial

When to plant: Spring and summer

Where to plant: They love a shady and moist spot. You can grow them in raised beds, buckets and on logs.

Size: This depends on the variety and the growing space you give to them.

How to grow: There are many different ways to grow mushrooms; each offer different levels of affordability, difficulty, time and quantity of mushrooms produced. Have a look at my chapter on growing mushrooms to find out all the different ways, but here I talk about growing them on logs.

Find a log from a healthy tree and avoid any that already have any pre-existing fungi otherwise you might find yourself growing some unwanted (and potentially dangerous) mushrooms. A diameter of no more than 30cm (12in) and length of no more than 1.5m (5ft) is ideal.

Once you have found the perfect log(s), you will want to start drilling holes for the spawn. About 50 holes for a 1.5m (5ft) log is enough. Drill 1.5cm (½in) holes along the length of the log; this depth will leave a small space on the inside of the log where plugs won't reach and this is where the mycelium will grow.

Begin the next row of holes about 5cm (2in) from the first line and make sure the holes don't line up but instead are drilled to the right (or left) of the above holes, creating a diamond-like pattern. Then you will want to lightly hammer the dowels into the holes; they should be just below the surface of the wood, allowing enough room to apply a wax seal on top. This step is very important as it's to prevent any damage being done and to prevent anything from infecting the mycelium. Any wax will do, so long as it stays in place and it's not toxic!

After all of the plugs are waxed, your log is ready for incubation. They're best kept somewhere shady with high humidity and good air circulation. If this isn't an option for you, you can cover them with a cloth. If winter where you live is particularly cold then store them inside your garage or a shed.

Wine Cap

The logs will need a soaking once or twice a week; if they ever dry up, no mushrooms will grow! So it's very important.

How to feed: Mushroom substrate

Common diseases and pests: Slugs and snails love to come and feast on mushrooms so use crushed up eggshells to make it difficult for them. You will see the tell tale slug trails!

How to harvest: Mushrooms that grow on logs will produce fruit once or twice a year for around four years with spring and autumn being the most common periods. Harvest your mushrooms as soon as you can as if you leave it too late they won't be as tasty and the texture will deteriorate.

MICROGREENS (PISUM SATIVUM)

I started growing microgreens when I first came to London because every time I went to a restaurant I was being served different dishes with a huge variety of microgreens and this piqued my interest. They are packed with nutrients and they come in many different varieties and flavours!

Recommended cultivars/varieties: Anything works! But most nutritious are Alfalfa, peas and amaranth

Perennial or annual: Annual

When to plant: All year round indoors

Where to plant: In a sunny spot on a windowsill or under lights to accelerate growth and increase yield.

Size: 2.5–7.5cm (1–3in) tall depending on the variety

How to grow: Pour one or two glasses of unchlorinated water into the bottom of a tray. Now fill the tray with soil or coco coir. Leave a 2.5cm (1in) gap at the top of the tray. Now evenly spread the seeds.

Mist the seeds with some water to trigger the germination process. The exception is things like peas which you need to soak in water before putting them on the soil to ensure a better germination rate. If you have boughts your seeds the instructions should tell you if you need to pre-soak them, otherwise have a quick google or ask an expert if not sure!

Leave them for two to three days to germinate and follow instructions depending on variety for growing.

Common diseases and pests: You have less to worry about than normal as these are grown indoors but look out for aphids and remove them or invite a ladybird in from the garden to feast on them.

How to harvest: Within two to three weeks of germination you should be able to harvest. You know that they are ready when you can see fully formed leaves appearing. Simply take a pair of scissors and snip them off just above the soil and: hey presto, you have microgreens.

Microgreens

NASTURTIUMS (TROPAEOLUM)

Not only are nasturtiums a beautiful companion plant, perfect for luring creepy crawlies and attracting bees, but the flowers, leaves and seeds are all edible, and a great addition to salads.

Recommended cultivars/varieties: Yeti, Fiery Festival

Perennial or annual: Annual

When to plant: Spring/summer

Where to plant: Sunny spot either in pots or straight into the ground, near to brassicas or beans.

Size: 30cm (12in)

How to grow: Sow the seeds in the spring where you want them to grow, in well-draining soil. You won't have to worry too much about the soil quality or watering except in particularly dry weather.

Water a well weeded and raked area before you sow, and simply push the seeds in with your finger about 1.5cm (½in) into the ground. Leave about 10cm (4in) between each seed and cover them with a thin layer of soil.

After a couple of weeks, thin out the weakest shoots so that you have a shoot every 30cm (12in). If you are planting in pots or containers, you might need to water occasionally, but otherwise, only in very dry conditions.

If you have a climbing type, you will want to support it with a cane or trellis.

Common diseases and pests: Nasturtiums are extremely susceptible to caterpillars and aphids, which is great if you want to lure them away from your other veg. It is a good idea to have a few plants growing, to increase the chance of having edible flowers, leaves and seeds to harvest.

How to harvest: Pick the flowers and leaves when they are still young and fresh, for a fantastic, peppery taste, not unlike watercress. The seed pods can be picked when still green and pickled to make a kind of caper.

Nasturtium

AMARANTH (AMARANTHUS)

This dramatic flowering plant will make your growing space look sensational, and with edible leaves and nutty seeds similar to quinoa, it's a fantastic addition to any growing space.

Recommended cultivars/varieties: Three-coloured amaranth

Perennial or annual: Annual

When to plant: Spring/summer

Where to plant: Sunny borders

Size: 60–100cm (2–3ft)

How to grow: Sow seeds indoors in early spring in moist compost, but don't cover. Use a propagator or clingfilm (plastic wrap) to retain moisture but let light in. Keep the germinating seeds at around 20°C (68°F). When you have saplings you will want to repot them, keeping them moist and in full sun until late spring.

After the threat of frost has passed, start getting them used to the outside by taking them out each day, before planting out in early summer, with each plant about 30cm (12in) apart.

If grown in the ground they will only need watering in very dry weather. Potted ones may need more watering.

Common diseases and pests: Although rare, aphids can transmit viruses to amaranth which will leave the leaves looking pale and unhealthy. If this happens the plant will need to be destroyed to stop its spread. Make sure you have plenty of ladybirds to keep the aphids down.

How to harvest: Fresh, young leaves are great raw in salads and older ones work well in a stir-fry. Towards the end of summer, the seeds will start to ripen and you can begin harvesting them. You can either shake the seed head over a bag or container, or leave it upside down for the seeds to fall away naturally.

Amaranth

SUNFLOWER (HELIANTHUS)

Sunflowers are little bursts of sunshine in the garden, and there is nothing like a growing competition to get children into planting and ignite their love of gardening.

Recommended cultivars/varieties: Teddy Bear, Goldie F1

Perennial or annual: Annual

When to plant: Spring

Where to plant: Direct sunlight

Size: 1.8–2.2m (6–7ft) tall!

How to grow: Sunflowers are great to grow from seed! Just pop them in some compost and gently push in a seed per cell. Then top off and water well. Leave in a warm, sunny spot indoors.

Once the seeds have grown to about 5cm (2in) you can pop them into individual pots. Water and leave them once again in a warm and sunny spot. When they are 30cm (12in) they are ready to be planted out in the garden. Just make sure the last frosts have passed.

Decide if you want to grow your sunflowers to produce lots of flowers or if you want to see how tall you can grow them! This will alter how you care for them. If growing for height, leave them to it. If you want to grow for the blooms, pinch them out to stunt the plant and allow it to focus on flowering. You will also want to stem the sunflower to support it, especially in winds and rain.

Common diseases and pests: Aphids – ladybirds are a brilliant way to keep these under control. Squirrels will also come and munch on them; thistles around the base can act as a deterrent and Americans will also have to contend with racoons.

White mould – make sure you have good circulation and drainage.

How to harvest: Harvest the seeds once the flower has died and turned brown. Tie a paper bag over the head to keep the birds away. Great for cooking, or store some to plant next year. Sunflower seeds can be stored for years!

BORAGE (BORAGO OFFICINALIS)

This beautiful plant has edible leaves and flowers, which taste a bit like cucumber, and so are a perfect addition to summer cocktails enjoyed in your garden.

Perennial or annual: Annual

When to plant: Spring

Where to plant: Full or partial sunlight with good drainage, near things like beans and peas.

Size: 90cm (35½in)

How to grow: Borage is best planted in the ground where you want it to grow, although it is possible to grow it in large containers. It doesn't like being transplanted, so it's best to choose a spot that has a decent amount of sun; dig a 5cm (2in) hole, pop a seed in before covering and watering.

Leave 30cm (12in) between each plant.

Once the plant starts to flower, you may want to deadhead it before the seeds develop, or you might end up with a garden full of borage the next year.

Common diseases and pests: Borage attracts insects, including bees and aphids, which is great for the other plants in your growing space.

How to harvest: Borage flowers are a great garnish for salads and drinks and should be picked as soon as they open. Young, tender leaves should be picked as soon as possible before they become too bitter and hairy.

CALENDULA (CALENDULA OFFICINALIS)

Not only do these beautiful flowers attract all sorts of pollinating insects, they're edible too, making fabulous garnishes for salads.

Recommended cultivars/varieties:

Pacific Mix, Orange Flush

Perennial or annual: Annual

When to plant: Spring/autumn

Where to plant: Partial sunlight, among other crops such as tomatoes and beans.

Size: 30cm (12in)

How to grow: Scatter the seeds amongst your other crops in mid-spring, dust with compost and water well. As seedlings start to appear, thin out to about 10cm (4in) apart. Water in dry conditions. Pick flowers continuously to encourage more growth, remembering to leave some toward the end of their life for seeds to plant the next year.

Common diseases and pests: None

How to harvest: Pick flowers as soon as they open.

MARIGOLD (TAGETES)

This beautiful, edible plant is a fantastically easy to grow companion plant that will not only liven up your salad, but also deter whitefly. An important note: some types of marigold are not edible, so please make sure you check before eating.

Recommended cultivars/varieties: African Mix, Yellow Inca II

Perennial or annual: Annual

When to plant: Spring/summer

Where to plant: Full sunlight borders, near tomatoes and cucumbers.

Size: 15–90cm (6–35½in)

How to grow: Sow seeds in small pots on your windowsill from early spring, or straight into the ground from late spring/early summer, leaving a 10–20cm (4–8in) gap between each plant.

If you are starting them off inside, you will want to get them used to the outside by putting them out during the day for a few weeks in late spring before planting them out permanently.

Watering is only really necessary in really dry weather unless in pots, and you will want to deadhead them to encourage new flowers.

Common diseases and pests: Marigolds can be susceptible to rot and mildew in damp conditions. Make sure that they are planted with good drainage, and there is plenty of space for air to circulate.

How to harvest: Pick young flowers and leaves when they are still fresh and vibrant. The flowers can be used to colour a dish, similar to saffron, as well as making a brilliant garnish.

LAVENDER (LAVANDULA)

Lavender is easy to grow and brings many bees to your garden; brilliant for pollination. It can even be used to make your own Herbes de Provence!

Recommended cultivars/varieties: Any French or Spanish variety

Perennial or annual: Perennial

When to plant: Spring

Where to plant: Sunny spot with well drained soil. I like to put it in places I walk past a lot in the garden to make the most of the smell! It is also beautiful in pots outside the front of your house. Just make sure your pots are well draining.

Size: Small to large bush

How to grow: You can grow lavender from seeds. It will take one to three months to germinate inside. The first year outside you won't get many flowers but your patience will be rewarded by year two. If you want to introduce pollinators to your garden to help establish other crops you can speed up the process by buying plugs or plants.

It is important to water lavender regularly in the first year of planting but after that you can relax a bit as it doesn't mind quite dry conditions.

It is important to prune your lavender in late summer after it has finished flowering otherwise it will become woody and it won't look great. It is best to remove about 2cm (1in) of the previous year's growth.

Common diseases and pests: The main issue is root rot due to being grown in heavy or wet soil. If you don't have the right soil in your garden, grow them in pots. Lavender attracts flies like rosemary beetles but they won't harm your plants so don't worry about this!

How to harvest: Pick lavender just before the flowers open to get the best fragrance. Hang them upside down to dry out and give them as gifts or to dot around your home.

Lavender

DAHLIA (DAHLIA)

They bring immense beauty and pleasure to the garden year on year. They look amazing in late summer and early autumn as they bring colour to the garden. All dahlias are edible and can vary in flavour from water chestnut to spicy apple flavour.

Recommended cultivars/varieties: Cafe au Lait, Bishop of York

Perennial or annual: Perennial

When to plant: Spring/summer

Where to plant: A warm, sunny, sheltered spot.

Size: They can grow to 1.5m (5ft) tall!

How to grow: You can germinate them from seed or grow them from a tuber. A greenhouse is the ideal place to start but you can use a sunny spot in your house before taking them outside after any frosts.

Allow only five shoots to grow from the tuber. It can feel a bit heavy handed but it will mean you get the best and most impressive flowers.

When you plant them outside, ensure you stake them, as wind and rain could break them. If you are growing them in a pot I suggest using a compact variety.

Make sure you pick the flowers or deadhead them to encourage lots of flowering! Just snip them off at the first green leaves you see under the flower.

Dahlias are perennial, but they are unlikely to survive a frost so you will need to decide if you will overwinter them in the ground with mulch or by lifting them.

Common diseases and pests: Earwigs – pop some pots full of straw underneath the plant. The earwigs go in there to get cosy; you can then move them elsewhere.

Slugs and snails – keep them away with coffee grounds or eggs shells.

How to harvest: It is tempting to pick the whole stem but snip them off to encourage new flowers. They keep going for ages if there are no frosts!

Dahlia

ZINNIA (ZINNIA)

The first flower to be grown in space by NASA – how cool is that. They have quite a bitter taste but are great in a salad or a cocktail and provide brilliant pops of colour to the garden.

Recommended cultivars/varieties:
Zinderella Peach

Perennial or annual: Annuals

When to plant: Summer

Where to plant: Sunny, well-drained spot. They can be grown in pots.

Size: from 15cm (6in) to 1m (3ft) depending on variety.

How to grow: Zinnias don't like being moved so it is best to plant them outside immediately or into a well-draining pot rather than trying to transplant them. It is really important to stake them to make sure they don't get damaged – if they do they won't flower.

They are thirsty plants and must not be allowed to dry out. It is best to water them at their roots and keep an extra special eye on them if they are in pots.

You can collect the seeds at the end of the season to save for next year.

Common diseases and pests: Botrytis is a fungus that will leave the leaves shrivelled and produce a fluffy grey mould. The best way to prevent this is to ensure good circulation. So be sure not to leave decaying leaves nearby. Also water the soil from the base, as overhead weathering will spread the fungus quicker.

How to harvest: Pick or deadhead them to ensure they keep flowering. They will look beautiful in your home or to share in a cocktail with friends.

Zinnia

SAGE (SALVIA OFFICINALIS)

Sage can last six to ten years in a bush. Its stunning edible purple flowers are great in salads or to add a pop of colour to a vinegar.

Recommended cultivars/varieties: Any variegated sage

Perennial or annual: Both

When to plant: Spring or autumn

Where to plant: A warm, sunny and sheltered spot. It can grow in dappled light but this will impact the flavour.

Size: 30–80cm (11¾–31½in)

How to grow: You can grow from seed, take cuttings from a friend or divide the plant (though not too often).

Seed: Scatter over the soil in a sunny spot that has good drainage. Cover with 3mm (⅛in) of compost and water well. It may take well over a month for the seeds to germinate. When they do, thin out and water often until roots have established.

Cutting: Take a cutting from new growth in the spring and dip it in root hormone before planting in a small pot and covering with a plastic bowl. Keep in a warm spot on a windowsill until it has visible growth, then repot or plant out.

Divide: If you know someone with an established plant, you can carefully dig up the root ball and, using a sharp knife, cut it in two. Replant both parts separately.

Common diseases and pests: Powdery mildew, which looks like someone has powdered the leaves! It is most likely to occur in early spring. Make sure your plant has enough water and circulation. Pluck the infected leaves and thin the plant for better circulation.

Rosemary beetle is a rather beautiful pest with its metallic green and purple body but it will strip your plant of its leaves. Check regularly and remove by hand and remove the larvae.

How to harvest: Pick the leaves all year round as it is evergreen but the best flavour is before the flowers. You can also harvest and eat the purple flowers. Strip back perennial varieties after the flowers have gone to ensure good regrowth next year.

MINT (MENTHA)

There are many different varieties of mint available and I am currently growing a few, including banana mint, chocolate mint, ginger mint, basil mint, lime mint, peppermint and my absolute favourite: pineapple mint.

Recommended cultivars/varieties:
Strawberry mint, Pineapple mint

Perennial or annual: Annual

When to plant: Spring

Where to plant: Mint thrives in pretty much any kind of moist, well draining and rich soil. It grows well in both full sun and partial shade. However if you live in a hot climate it is recommended to grow it in partial shade.

Avoid growing different varieties of mint close together either in pots or in the ground. They could lose their individual flavours and scents. A few years ago I made the mistake of planting mint straight in the ground in the only spot of open ground that I have in my garden. It took over the whole space and trying to control it was absolutely pointless. I had to remove all the existing plants and dig up roughly 1m (3ft) of soil and sift through it. The reason is that mint roots spread easily because of the rhizomes. Rhizome is a large underground stem that grows horizontally and shoots out roots and new shoots.

This means that even if a small bit of root is still in the ground it will develop new shoots. This is why you should always grow mint in isolation or in containers.

Size: Small bush

How to grow: Sow your mint seeds in a pot by sprinkling them over the surface and lightly covering them with soil. You don't want it to be too dense as they need light to germinate. Keep them watered and you should be able to harvest them in three months. Don't forget to repot them as they grow and keep them away from other mint varieties!

Water mint regularly and keep the soil moist but not soaking wet.

Mint is a plant that grows really dense and sometimes much more than we can consume. Don't worry even if you don't use it straight away, it is recommended to prune it down and store it for later use. You should always prune back lateral shoots and chop off a few nodes. Your mint will benefit from pruning especially at the end of the season when the plant is due to go dormant.

I usually prune it down to pretty much ground level at the end of the season. Then the next season it will come back even stronger. This is also

Mint

a great chance to clone your mint and make many more plants.

How to feed: Feed your mint with an organic fertilizer like well rotted manure or a slow release fertilizer like insect frass or worm casting. You should start feeding your mint when spring begins or roughly one month after you have planted it.

Common diseases and pests: There are lots of pests that could attack your mint e.g. mites and aphids.

If you have a light infestation you could spray your plants with a jet of water and this will get rid of the aphids. As a last resort, insecticides might be needed if the infestation is strong. Look for insecticides with imidacloprid; this will kill the aphids without killing any other beneficial insects like bees and butterflies.

I also tried nematodes as a preventive measure or at the first sign of a light infestation. You could simply mix it with water and directly water the base of the mint plant or spray the leaves. I noticed that two applications of nematodes one month apart drastically reduced the amount of pests attacking my plants. Natural predators like lacewings or ladybirds could be attracted or even released at the beginning of the season so you will have organic pest control in your garden; make sure to source native predators.

How to harvest: Snip off stems or leaves as and when you need it. If you are cutting it back you can dry it easily, or infuse it into vinegar or oil, or even whizz it up and freeze it.

PARSLEY (PETROSELINUM CRISPUM)

Parsley is one of the most common herbs used in Italian cooking. It is also a breath freshener and often gets paired with garlic.

Perennial or annual: Annual

When to plant: Spring

Where to plant: It can grow in part shade so it is a great one for your borders.

Size: Small bush

How to grow: The key to success with parsley is to plant more seeds than you need! Not all will germinate and for best results soak them in warm water for 36 hours to remove the preventive coating.

Parsley loves moist and warm conditions so, if you don't have a greenhouse, cover your pots with a plastic bag until they germinate. Then remove and pop them in a sunny spot in your house. Make sure you thin them out so the strongest survive and then harden them off before planting them outside.

If you are growing in a pot make sure it is deep to allow for its roots and you give it plenty of water. Pick parsley to encourage growth through the season.

Common diseases and pests: Carrot fly – a small black fly whose larvae feast on the roots of the parsley. There isn't much you can do once they arrive so prevention is key! Be careful not to crush the parsley as the smell attracts them. Plant them with companion plants like chives and garlic to mask the smell and don't plant them near your carrots.

Aphids – these greenfly are seen on the leaves of the plant. Ladybirds love aphids, so buy some for a natural solution.

How to harvest: Snip the parsley near the base and use it for cooking. If you want to keep some for the winter you can preserve it by drying or popping it into ice cubes.

Parsley

BASIL (OCIMUM BASILICUM)

As an Italian, I can't get enough basil: in tomato salad, on pizza or pasta sauce, or served as a pesto. It's easy to grow too, and a great companion plant for – you've guessed it – tomatoes.

Recommended cultivars/varieties: Genovese, Thai basil, Purple basil

Perennial or annual: Annual

When to plant: Spring/summer

Where to plant: Does great on a windowsill out of direct sunlight, or as a companion plant with tomatoes, chillies and asparagus.

Size: Small bush

How to grow: Start planting the seeds in trays in spring on a shady but warm windowsill in early spring. The compost should remain moist, but never waterlogged. Once you have seedlings you can plant them into individual pots, keeping them warm and moist.

Once the frost has gone, you can start putting the pots outside during the day to replant in early summer, or repot as they grow.

If you keep harvesting from them and don't allow them to bolt, you can bring them in in autumn and keep harvesting.

Common diseases and pests: The main problem for basil is slugs and snails if growing in or near to the ground. Use crushed up eggshells to make it difficult for them.

How to harvest: Pick leaves as and when you need them. Don't use scissors as this inhibits growth.

Basil

ROSEMARY (SALVIA ROSMARINUS)

A versatile herb that looks fantastic and smells incredible. It's an amazing addition to any growing space, especially in spring when it's in flower.

Recommended cultivars/varieties:
Barbeque

Perennial or annual: Perennial

When to plant: Spring/autumn

Where to plant: Sunny, sheltered spots with plenty of drainage.

Size: Can grow into quite a large bush.

How to grow: Sow seeds indoors in early spring if you have a propagator, or in late spring on a windowsill. Use a tray or individual pots with moist compost and sprinkle the seeds on top. Dust a thin layer of compost on top and cover with a clear plastic bowl or some cling film (plastic wrap).

Once the seeds have germinated and you have saplings you will want to repot them into bigger pots. You really want the drainage to be good, so you will want to put some small stones under the compost when you do this. It is important that the roots don't get waterlogged.

As the rosemary grows, repot as necessary, until early summer, when you can take the plant outside. If you want to plant permanently outside, make sure the area you choose is sunny and has excellent drainage. You might want to dig away clay rich soil, add some stones or gravel and then add compost before planting.

Harvest regularly and prune back once a year in winter to prevent the plant from becoming too woody.

Common diseases and pests: The most common problem with growing rosemary is insufficient drainage. If you have trouble growing it in the ground, try using pots with plenty of stones in the bottom.

How to harvest: Pick the newest growth as and when you need it.

How to clone/propagate: Snip a freshly grown stem that's about 15–20cm (5–7in) and remove most of the lower leaves. Cut the bottom of the stem off just below the leaf node (knobbly bit that the leaves grow from) and dip it into some rooting powder. Stick the stem into a flower pot with stones for drainage and compost. Keep it moist, but not too wet.

OREGANO *(ORIGANUM VULGARE)*

Oregano is a great, Mediterranean herb that I use a lot in my Italian cooking. It's pretty easy to grow, smells great in your garden and looks beautiful when in flower.

Perennial or annual: Perennial

When to plant: Spring

Where to plant: Sunny, sheltered spot, great for ground cover.

Size: Can grow to a medium-sized bush.

How to grow: Sprinkle a few seeds on the top of some good, moist but well-drained compost in early spring. Keep it in a warm place like a sunny windowsill and make sure that the soil remains moist but not waterlogged.

When you have some saplings, repot them, keeping them in the warm place until late spring. They may need repotting again unless you plan on planting it out. If so, wait until the threat of frost has gone, before acclimatizing them by putting them out during the day for a week or so.

Plant them in a sunny, sheltered spot with very good drainage. You might want to throw in a handful of gravel as you plant them. Water sparingly unless kept in pots or in particularly dry weather where you should water more regularly. Harvest often.

Cut your oregano right back in the middle of summer to encourage new growth, and if kept in pots, repot once every year or so in the springtime.

Common diseases and pests: As long as you have good drainage you shouldn't have any problems.

How to harvest: Pinch new growth off as and when you need it. Prune right back in midsummer and dry the leaves in the sun.

Oregano

CHIVES (ALLIUM SCHOENOPRASUM)

Not only do chives have the most stunning flowers, they are super tasty and so easy to grow, both outside and on a windowsill.

Recommended cultivars/varieties: Garlic chives, and if you have a bit more space Siberian chives

Perennial or annual: Perennial

When to plant: Spring

Where to plant: Full sunshine or partial shade.

Size: 30cm (12in)

How to grow: Start sowing the seeds in early spring if you have a heated propagator at 20–25°C (68-77°F), or late spring if using a windowsill. Either way, sprinkle the seeds on top of moist, well drained soil and let them grow for three weeks.

When you have some saplings you will want to repot them into small pots. Keep the soil moist, and gently acclimatize them to the outside if you are going to plant them out in late spring. If so, they will want a sunny or partially shaded spot with good drainage.

Being perennial, chives will come back and even multiply year after year. You might want to thin them out and declump them when they do this, especially if grown in pots.

Common diseases and pests: Wet/humid conditions can lead to leek rust, which is a fungus that causes bright yellow spots on the leaves. There is no cure, so if your chives get it they need to be destroyed, but not composted as it could spread. Also, avoid growing other alliums, such as onions or leeks, in the same area.

How to harvest: Snip off the leaves from the base as and when you want to use them. Snip off the flowers from the top of the stem.

Chives

THYME (THYMUS VULGARIS)

Thyme is one of the most versatile herbs; it's easy to grow and can look beautiful too, especially when its stunning flowers come into bloom.

Recommended cultivars/varieties: Lemon thyme, Creeping thyme (this spreads well and can even replace your lawn!)

Perennial or annual: Perennial

When to plant: Spring/autumn

Where to plant: Sunny, sheltered spot with good drainage.

Size: around 25cm (10in)

How to grow: Sow seeds indoors in early spring if you have a propagator, or in late spring on a windowsill. Use a tray or individual pots with moist compost and sprinkle the seeds on top. Dust a thin layer of compost on top and cover with a clear plastic bowl or some cling film (plastic wrap).

Once the seeds have germinated and you have saplings you will want to repot them into bigger pots. You really want the drainage to be good, so you will want to put some small stones under the compost when you do this. It is important that the roots don't get waterlogged.

As the thyme grows, repot as necessary, until late summer, when you can take the plant outside. If you want to plant permanently outside, make sure the area you choose is sunny and has excellent drainage. You might want to dig away clay-rich soil, add some stones or gravel and then add compost before planting. Thyme will grow well on gravel, or even in cracks on walls and pavements.

Common diseases and pests: The main problem thyme faces is being over-watered. Once it is established it doesn't need watering, and will benefit from being taken indoors over winter, especially if wet.

How to harvest: Snip off the leaves and flowers as and when you need them.

Thyme

STRAWBERRIES IN A POT (FRAGARIA ANANASSA)

Strawberries are like sweets of the summer, and there is nothing like homegrown ones. They are easy to grow in pots or hanging baskets and can look very pretty too.

Recommended cultivars/varieties: Choose based on your climate and whether you want early or late production

Perennial or annual: Perennial

When to plant: Spring/summer

Where to plant: Direct sun

Size: Small bush

How to grow: You will need one big, deep pot with good drainage (a layer of gravel at the bottom works well) per strawberry plant, filled with high quality, moist fertilizer. If you are growing from runners, get these in early spring; if from plants, wait until early summer.

Keep the soil moist, avoid getting the plant wet and feed weekly with tomato feed. Once it has stopped producing fruit, cut back so it can regrow next year. You should get at least two years of fruit before they need replacing.

Common diseases and pests: Slugs, snails and birds are common problems for strawberries. You could put some straw down around the plant to deter slugs and snails. This will also help to suppress weeds and keep the soil warm. Netting prevents birds from stealing strawberries.

Grey mould can affect strawberries in damp conditions. Keep the plant as dry as possible, watering only the soil in the morning. If you see an affected fruit, dispose of it before it spreads.

How to clone/propagate: Strawberries produce runners, which can create whole new plants. While the plant is in full fruit production, snip these off so all the energy goes into creating strawberries. Once the fruit begins to dwindle you can allow runners to grow. When this happens, keeping it attached to the parent plant, place it on top of a pot filled with compost and pin it down with some garden wire.

Keeping the soil moist and the new plant attached to the old, wait for it to establish strong roots before you snip it and repot it. You can do this every year for an endless supply.

RASPBERRIES IN A POT (RUBUS IDAEUS)

Raspberries are so easy and cheap to grow, yet buying them can be quite expensive. Growing in pots means that anyone can enjoy them, no matter the growing space.

Recommended cultivars/varieties: Choose based on your climate and whether you want early or late production

Perennial or annual: Perennial

When to plant: Autumn for seeds, spring for cane

Where to plant: Sunny spot

Size: 2–3m (7–9ft) tall

How to grow: Raspberry plants are often bought in cane form, either as "bare root" or in containers, but can be grown from seed quite easily. You can buy seeds, or simply sieve them out of store-bought raspberries and leave them on a paper towel to dry.

Plant the seeds in a tray of moist compost in the autumn about 6mm (¼ in) deep, 2.5cm (1in) apart. Put the seeds outside, either in a cold frame, or an unheated room, like a shed or garage. This will help the seeds to germinate.

In the spring, when the air temperature is around 16°C (60°F) you can move the tray outside to a partially shaded area. Meanwhile, prepare your pots for planting by making sure that it has good drainage and rich compost. If your variety is summer fruiting you will need a cane to support it too. Once the saplings are 2.5cm (1in) tall you can start repotting them. They will need about 60–90cm (23½–35½in) each, so unless you have very large pots, one per pot.

Common diseases and pests: You might want to cover your raspberries in netting to prevent birds, mice and other small animals from accessing them.

How to harvest: If grown from seed, it can take up to 18 months to produce fruit. When it does, pick carefully and often.

Raspberries

WATERMELON (CITRILLUS LANATUS)

You can grow a watermelon in pretty much any shape you want! While a watermelon is still small on the vine, place a tempered transparent glass shape round it e.g. a square one. As your watermelon grows it will grow into the shape of the glass. Square- and heart-shaped watermelons are really popular in Japan.

Recommended cultivars/varieties: Best for small spaces is Melon Champagne F1

Perennial or annual: Annual

When to plant: Spring/summer

Where to plant: Watermelons love sun and well-drained spots! You can grow them in a greenhouse, under cloches or a cold frame. You can even grow them in a pot on your balcony – just make sure the pot is big enough! I would recommend choosing a compact watermelon in a small space. You can even train them to grow on a trellis.

To help reduce pests, marigolds and nasturtiums make great companions.

Size: Dependent on the variety. It makes sense to work out how much space you have first and then choose your variety.

How to grow: You can save watermelon seeds and store them for five years but they may not give you the same variety! Start your seeds inside and transplant them outside after the last frost and when the ground has warmed up. Watermelons are vines that like to spread out so be

sure you have space! If you decide to train them to grow up a trellis, think about how you will support the vine and the fruit. You will need to make hammocks for the fruit – you can use old t-shirts to do this.

Common diseases and pests: Powdery mildew – ensure your plant has enough water and circulation. This will likely occur in early spring. Pluck the infected leaves and thin the plant for better circulation.

Melon Aphids, also known as cotton aphids, make their homes under the leaves and feast on the sap. A great way to control them is to introduce ladybirds or lacewings to your garden.

How to harvest: When ready to harvest, the skin of the watermelon will turn from shiny to dull. If you look at the underside you will see it turns light green or yellow.

MELON *(CUCUMIS MELO)*

Did you know there are over 1,200 varieties of melon? The most expensive melons in the world are the Japanese Yubari King Melons; they can sell for over $20,000!

Recommended cultivars/varieties:
Eich Sweetness

Perennial or annual: Annual

When to plant: Late spring/summer

Where to plant: A sunny spot with humidity. If you are in a colder climate, grow them in a greenhouse, polytunnel, under a cloche or in a coldframe. You can grow a melon on a balcony in a pot and for best results choose a dwarf variety.

They can cross breed with other plants like squash or cucumber so it is best not to plant them near them!

Size: Dependent on variety from dwarf melons to big juicy ones!

How to grow: Start your melons inside as they are very sensitive to temperature and a frost will kill them off. It is best to harden your seeds indoors first. Then sow a couple of seeds in a pot and leave to germinate. Remove the weakest seedlings and plant once the last chance of frost has passed. Don't panic if you don't see any fruit after the first flowers – melons normally flower twice before producing fruit. You will need to train your vines and also pinch out the growing point at the fifth leaf to encourage side shoots. Keep the strongest side shoots and remove the others!

As the melons begin to grow you want to choose the strongest four on each stem and remove the others – you can do this when they are the size of a small egg.

How to feed: Potash works really well to help melons grow especially in cooler climates.

Common diseases and pests: Powdery mildew which looks like someone has powdered the leaves! It is most likely to occur in early spring. Make sure your plant has enough water and circulation. Pluck the infected leaves and thin the plant for better circulation.

Melon aphids, also known as cotton aphids, make their homes under the leaves and feast on the sap. A great way to control them is to introduce ladybirds or lacewings to your garden.

How to harvest: Smell them! The sweet scent of melon lets you know they are ready to be enjoyed. Just pluck them from the vine. If you reduce the amount you water them when they are almost ripe, they provide a sweeter melon.

DWARF FRUIT TREES (URBAN ORCHARD)

Dwarf fruit trees are simply smaller versions of trees that are easier to manage and maintain, especially in a smaller plot of land. The best part of growing dwarf varieties is that you can grow them in pots and this is what I do in my garden!

Perennial or annual: Perennial

When to plant: Trees should be planted when they are dormant, i.e. in winter or early spring. This gives the tree a chance to regrow the roots that have been pruned or lost in transplanting. If you haven't planted your orchard come April, the trees won't have a chance to grow roots and will find it difficult to establish themselves. It would be better to wait until December when they go back to dormancy.

Where to plant: A sheltered, southwest-facing plot is ideal for most fruit trees as it will be exposed to the most sunlight and protected from the harshest weather. A walled or enclosed courtyard could work well. However "rain shadows" must be taken into account, especially if the tree is using the walls for support. The walls tend to dry out at the bottom, even in wet weather, so an irrigation system is vital.

Size: Most dwarf trees will grow to about 2.5–3m (8–10ft) tall

Dwarf Apple Tree

Dwarf Peach Tree

How to grow: Remember when selecting your trees that as they grow they will need space to spread out. Try to avoid buying more mature trees as you are likely to inherit a myriad of problems. Instead, buy healthy 2–3-year-old trees. You might have to wait a year or two before your first crop, but at least they will come problem-free.

Traditionally, orchards are planted in a grid system, with rows of trees running north to south, maximizing exposure to the sun. This however, is not essential, and the size and shape of your plot will determine your layout. On the other hand, sufficient spacing is essential, and will ultimately be determined by the size of your trees once fully grown. Dwarf trees should be at least 3.5m (11½ft) apart, semi-dwarf at least 5m (16ft). This will ensure sufficient exposure to sun and minimize root competition.

The best time to transplant your trees is early spring, after the main frost, and before it stops being dormant. Prune the tree prior to transplanting to minimize loss of water and encourage new growth.

Once planted, new trees will require regular watering; it will depend on the weather and will encourage root growth, giving them a better chance of establishing themselves. They also respond well to straw-based organic manure.

Common diseases and pests: Poor drainage can be potentially disastrous for most fruit trees. Symptoms of this are poor growth, discoloured leaves, defoliation (loss of leaves) and thinning of the crown (the part of the tree above ground). The best way to prevent this is to make sure that water can drain away sufficiently.

If you do get an abundance of aphids, it is likely that it will soon be followed by an army of hungry ladybirds. Waiting for this to happen might be detrimental though, especially with young trees. Luckily, you can easily and cheaply buy boxes of live ladybirds to do the pest control work for you.

Other pests, such as caterpillars, slugs and beetles can be removed by hand; or, like the aphids and ladybirds, will naturally attract their own predators, thereby creating a biodiverse ecosystem.

Diseases, such as apple canker, brown rot and grey mould are rare, but if left unchecked, could be lethal to the plant. By removing fallen leaves and fruit you are reducing the risk of these from infecting the plant in the first place. If they appear, simply pruning away the infected area should remove the problem and allow air to circulate.

How to harvest: Pick the fruit when ripe depending on variety.

INDEX

PICTURE CREDITS

The following photographs are copyright © Shutterstock 2023: 57 (both images), 88, 89, 124, 129, 174 (both images), 175, 176, 180, 181, 183 (the vine weevil image), 222, 226, 230, 237, 240, 241, 244, 252, 256, 257, 259, 260, 261, 263, 264

The illustrations on page 2, part openers and chapter openers are also copyright © Shutterstock 2023